The Complete
Ninja Foodi
PossibleCooker Cookbook for Beginners

Simple and Selected Ninja PossibleCooker Recipes to
Help You Use Ninja Foodi PossibleCooker PRO

Bernice Cochran

CONTENT

Introduction

Cooking is the best part of everyone's life. Cooking delicious food with your family makes your time memorable. Everyone wants to eat delicious and healthy food that should be cooked in less time. You will think how is that possible? Yes! It is possible due to Ninja Foodi PossibleCooker PRO cooking appliance. The Ninja Foodi PossibleCooker PRO makes life easy because you can cook your favorite food using different cooking functions. This cooking appliance is perfect for your family. You can easily understand the buttons of the control panel. The cleaning process is also super easy.

Ninja Foodi PossibleCooker PRO will take less time to prepare mouthwatering meals. If you have no time to cook your favorite food, the Ninja Foodi PossibleCooker PRO will help you cook different meals using different cooking functions. My cookbook included delicious Ninja Foodi PossibleCooker PRO recipes for you. You can cook these dishes with your cooking appliance easily. The method of using Ninja Foodi PossibleCooker PRO is super easy. I will give instructions on how it will use. I will guide you on "how to use Ninja Foodi PossibleCooker PRO cooking appliance"? How many buttons does it have? How cooking functions work, and many more! You will get answers to every question that comes to your mind. In my cookbook, you will get simple delicious that have step-by-step cooking instructions and easy-to-find ingredients.

Ninja Foodi PossibleCooker PRO will save you time. Prepare your ingredients according to the recipe instructions and add them to the cooking pot using desired cooking functions. Adjust the temperature and cooking time according to the recipe instructions. You will get mouthwatering meals on your table on weekend dinner in less time. Make your time memorable by cooking food in Ninja Foodi PossibleCooker PRO. It will not disappoint you.

Ninja Foodi PossibleCooker PRO has multiple cooking modes. You can choose your favorite mode according to food requirements and start cooking different meals for your family and friends.

What is Ninja Foodi PossibleCooker PRO?

Ninja Foodi PossibleCooker PRO is a unique cooking appliance. It has eight cooking functions. These are the followings: Slow cook, Sear or Sauté, Braise, Sous Vide, Steam, Bake, Proof, and Keep Warm. These cooking functions are super easy to use. I will guide you on how it works. You can select cooking functions according to food like vegetables, protein, fruits, and many more. Prepare your favorite dishes for special occasions. For example: If you want to eat cookies, cakes, bars, blondies, and pies, you can choose the bake cooking function for these dishes. If you want to eat a crispy and salty dish, choose sear or sauté cooking mode. Keep warm is a necessary cooking function because if your food becomes cold, you can reheat it using the keep warm cooking mode.

Cooking Functions

Slow Cook	Steam
Sear or Sauté	Bake
Braise	Proof
Sous Vide	Keep Warm

Slow cook: You can prepare meat, protein, and soups using this cooking function. It takes a lot of time to cook food, but it gives you delicious food. You can adjust the cooking time and go to work.You will have a delicious meal with great taste when you return.

Steam: Everyone loves steamed food. Using this cooking mode, you can cook delicate food at high temperatures. Examples: Fish, lamb, eggs, mushrooms, spinach, and seaweed. Steam cooking mode eliminates the extra oils from the food and keeps it moist.

Sear or Sauté: When you start cooking veggies, choose a sear or sauté button to give a crispy taste to the meals. You can cook mushroom stir-fry, broccoli, roasted cauliflower, and many more.

Bake: Everyone loves to bake food like cookies, donuts, cake, pies, bars, blondies, muffins, cupcakes, and many more. You can prepare special treats at home for special occasions using this cooking mode.

Braise: Bring restaurant-style meals at home using the Braise cooking function. Using this cooking mode, you can prepare Braise beef, Braise chicken, Eggplant stew, and veggies.

Proof: Proof cooking mode provides low heat to maintain the environment to raise the dough or yeast. For Example, Cookie dough, brownie dough, and many more. You can use it for making bread.

Sous Vide: The Sous vide method is the perfect choice for cooking food. It is a process of sealing food into an air-tight container. It yields a delicious taste and is perfect for making tender meats and veggies.

Keep warm: It is an essential cooking mode for food. If your food is getting cold, you can easily reheat it. It will maintain the taste of food. You can use it after cooking the meal to keep your food warm.

There are a lot of benefits of using Ninja Foodi PossibleCooker PRO cooking appliances. Some are given below:

Easy-to-Make Different Meals

With Ninja Foodi PossibleCooker PRO cooking appliance, you can cook your favorite meals such as beef, chicken, leg of lamb, fresh and frozen veggies, fruits, desserts, snacks, appetizers, and many more. Every type of meal you want to cook on your special days. This cooking appliance is super convenient. Cook meals filled with yummy tastes.

Easy Cleaning Process

Many people didn't know how to clean the parts of Ninja Foodi appliances and got worried, but now you don't need to confuse about it. You will find whole guidance about cleaning methods. I added step-by-step instructions about the cleaning process for Ninja Foodi possible cooker pro. Read it below. Note: Don't use harsh chemicals to clean it. It can damage your appliance.

Multiple Cooking Functions

The Ninja Foodi PossibleCooker PRO cooking appliance has eight different cooking functions: These are the followings: Slow cook, Sear or Sauté, Braise, Sous Vide, Steam, Bake, Proof, and Keep Warm. You can select your favorite cooking mode onto the equipment and prepare your favorite food.

Endless Possibilities in One Pot

Ninja Foodi PossibleCooker PRO makes everything possible. Sauté your food to get perfection, toss all ingredients and get pretty and tasty food, bake your food, and serve straight. Get compliments from your family and friends. How amazing is this pot! Pretty simple to use!

Before First Use the Ninja Foodi PossibleCooker PRO

Step: 1

Remove and discard any packaging material, tape, and stickers from the cooking appliance.

Step: 2

Take out all accessories from the box and read this manual carefully. You should pay attention to warnings, important safeguards, and operational instructions to avoid any injury or damage.

Step: 3

Rinse the Main Base Unit, Inner cooking pot, cooking pot lid, and Spoon–ladle with a damp and soapy cloth, then wash with a clean damp cloth and dry completely. Don't submerge the main unit in water.

Step: 4

Turn on the unit and run it for 10 minutes without adding ingredients. Make sure that area is ventilated well. It will discard any residue and odor from the unit. It is completely safe for Ninja Foodi PossibleCooker PRO.

These are essential parts and accessories of this appliance. For cooking food, you need to use these accessories. These are the followings:

Spoon-Ladle: Ninja Foodi PossibleCooker PRO come with a unique thing. Spoon-Ladle is used to add ingredients to the pot. You can use it to stir the ingredients while cooking food.

Top Pot Handle Or Spoon-Ladle Rest: It handles the spoon ladle.

Cooking Lid: It is used to cover the pot. It has a handle at the top. You can hold it easily to open or close the pot.

Side Pot Handles: These handles are at the sides of the cooking pot. You can hold it to handle the cooking pot.

Cooking Pot: The size of this cooking pot is 8.5 Quart. Add all ingredients to it and close it with a lid. Start cooking!

Side Pot Handles: These are at the side of the unit pot. You can hold it easily and lift it out.

Main Unit: Ninja Foodi PossibleCooker PRO has a control panel and handle.

Control Panel: The control panel has a screen which tells about cooking time and temperature. You can choose cooking functions also after scrolling the buttons.

There are eight cooking functions in the appliance. You can select one of these cooking modes and prepare your favorite food.

Slow Cook

Slow cook cooking mode is a perfect choice if you are a busy mom and have no time to cook your favorite food. If you didn't want to stand in the kitchen for a whole day, Ninja Foodi PossibleCooker PRO is best for you. It cooks food at very low heat but takes a long time to cook. It takes a long time to cook, but it gives a delicious taste to the food. You can adjust the cooking time and go to sleep. The next day, you will get delicious food. You can cook soups, meats, stews, and tender veggies using a slow cooking function.

Sear/Sauté

Sear or Sauté cooking mode is the same as cooking meals on the stovetop in the pan or Crockpot. Each meal needs this cooking mode to give a crispy taste to food. You can use this cooking mode for sautéing veggies, browning meats, simmering sauces, and many more. It is super easy to use. Prepare delicious lunch and dinner using this cooking mode.

Braise

Using Braise cooking mode, you can prepare food at high heat with oil and then simmer it in the liquid at low heat. Braise is a good choice for preparing Swiss steak, pot roast, coq au vin, sauerbraten, beef bourguignon, beef brisket, oxtail, tajines, beef short ribs and chuck, pork shoulder and Boston butt, lamb shoulder and shanks, chicken thighs and legs, and many more.

Sous Vide

Sous vide is a unique cooking method. The word "Sous vide" means under vacuum. It is a process of vacuum-sealing meals into the bag and cooking them at a precise temperature in the water bath. It is a process of sealing food into an air-tight container. You will get perfect and delicious meals. The best things you can cook using sous vide cooking mode are the followings: Egg, fish, lamb, carrots, liver, and fillet steak.

Steam

Steamed food is easily digested. Using steam cooking mode, you can prepare yummy meals. You can cook delicate food at high temperatures. For example, you can cook salmon, mushrooms, eggs, seaweed, and spinach. Steam cooking mode eliminates the extra oils from the food and keeps it moist.

Bake

Using bake cooking mode, prepare sweet and savory meals. Everyone loves baking food. You can prepare cookies, cake, brownies, pies, casseroles, squares, bars, loaves of bread, doughnuts, rolls, muffins, cupcakes, pizza, and many more. I added baking recipes to my cookbook. You can select your favorite and start preparing it using Ninja Foodi PossibleCooker PRO cooking appliance.

Proof

Proof cooking mode provides low heat to maintain the environment to raise the yeast/dough. For example, grow the dough for bread, brownies, cookies, and many more.

Keep Warm

Keep Warm cooking mode is the essential mode for you. You can keep your food warm after cooking it. Reheat your favorite food. It will not change the taste of the meals like a stovetop. Keep your food warm until serving.

Buttons and User Guide of Ninja Foodi PossibleCooker PRO

The control panel has these essential buttons for cooking meals. Here, I will guide you on which button is used for what purpose.

Power: The power button is used to open and close the unit and all cooking modes.

Temperature Arrows: This arrow is used to adjust the cooking temperature. Use the up and down arrows to adjust the cooking temperature of your food. In the recipe, the cooking temperature is mentioned. You can select the temperature according to the recipe instructions.

Time Arrows: This arrow is used to adjust the cooking time. Use the up and down arrows to adjust the cooking time for your food. In the recipe, cooking time is mentioned. You can select cooking time according to the recipe instructions.

Start/Stop Button: The start/stop button is used to start the cooking. Press the start/stop button while cooking meals to stop the current cooking mode. Select another cooking mode and again press the start/stop button to start the cooking again.

Function Dial: This unit offers eight cooking functions. Use the dial to choose the cooking function. Select your favorite cooking mode to start cooking meals.

Using the Ninja Foodi PossibleCooker PRO

COOKING FUNCTIONS: How to use it?

Slow Cook

☼ To turn on the unit: Press the power button.

☼ Open the cooking lid.

☼ Add the required ingredients into the cooking pot.

☼ According to the recipe instructions, add the required ingredients to the pot and close the lid.

☼ Use the dial button and select the cooking mode "SLOW COOK."

☼ Use the +/- temperature arrows to choose the HI or LO. You can choose the temperature according to the recipe instructions.

☼ Choose the cooking time between three to twelve hours in fifteen minutes increments. You can choose the cooking time according to the recipe instructions.

☼ Press the start/stop button to start cooking. When the cooking time reaches zero, the cooking appliance will beep and automatically turn to KEEP WARM mode and start counting up.

NOTE: SLOW COOK LO time can be adjusted between six to twelve hours. On the other hand, SLOW COOK HI time can be adjusted between three to twelve hours. You can select HI or LO time according to the recipe instructions. It is mentioned in the recipe.

Sear/Sauté

☼ To turn on the unit: Press the power button.

☼ Use the dial button and select the cooking mode "SEAR/SAUTE."

☼ Use the +/- temperature arrows to choose the HI or LO. You can choose the temperature according to the recipe instructions.

☼ Allow the appliance to preheat for five minutes before adding the ingredients.

☼ Open the cooking lid.

☼ Add the required ingredients into the cooking pot.

☼ According to the recipe instructions, add the required ingredients to the pot and close the lid.

☼ Press the start/stop button to start cooking. The timer will count up to keep track of

cooking time.

☼ Press the start/stop button to turn off the sear/sauté cooking mode and dial to choose the STEAM cooking mode.

NOTE: Don't use metal utensils for cooking because they will scratch the non-stick coating from the pot. Your pot will damage. You can use this cooking mode with or without a lid on the pot.

Steam

☼ To turn on the unit: Press the power button.

☼ Use the dial button and select the cooking mode "STEAM."

☼ Use the +/- time arrows to choose or adjust the cooking time in one-minute increments.

☼ Press the start/stop button to start cooking. The display screen will show "PRE", indicating the unit is preheating to the selected temperature.

☼ When the unit reaches the appropriate steam level, the display will show to adjust the temperature, and the timer will begin to count down. You can choose the temperature according to the recipe instructions.

☼ When the cooking time reaches zero, the cooking appliance will beep, and the display screen will show "END." The cooking appliance automatically turns to KEEP WARM cooking mode at the end of each cooking function.

NOTE: Add more cups of water or liquid to the pot when steaming.

Keep Warm

Use the dial to choose the "KEEP WARM" cooking function. Temperature will default and the appliance will begin counting up.

NOTE:

You can adjust the time and temperature by using +/- button in one minute increments up to one hour or five minutes increment up to 6 hours.

Sous Vide

☼ To turn on the unit: Press the power button.

☼ Then, add twelve cups of room temperature water to the cooking pot. Close the lid.

☼ Use the dial button and select the cooking mode "SOUS VIDE."

☼ The default temperature will show onto the screen.

☼ Use the +/- temperature arrow to adjust the temperature in five degrees increment between 120 degrees Fahrenheit to 190 degrees Fahrenheit. You can select the temperature according to the recipe instructions.

☼ The cooking time will default to three hours. Use the +/- cooking time arrow to adjust the cooking time in 15 minutes increment up to 12 hours or 1 minute increment from 12 to 24 hours. You can select the cooking time according to the recipe instructions.

☼ The display will show "PRE" onto the screen and current temperature showing preheat is in progress.

☼ When preheating is completed, the display will show "ADD FOOD" onto screen. Add ingredients into the pot. Close the lid. After a half minute, the unit will start counting down from the preset cook time.

NOTE: Sous vide cooking mode is always the first step in the cooking process. Food should be completed by using a dry heat method for example air frying, roasting, sautéing, and broiling, etc.

Braise

☼ To turn on the unit: Press the power button.

☼ Add ingredients into the pot using sear or sauté cooking instructions. When it completed, deglaze the pot with stock or wine.

☼ NOTE: To deglaze, add one cup of stock or wine into the cooking pot. Scrape the brown bits from bottom and sides of the cooking pot and combine into the cooking liquid.

☼ After that, add remaining liquid and ingredients into the pot.

☼ Use the dial button and select the cooking mode "BRAISE."

☼ The default temperature will show onto the screen. Use the +/- time arrows to adjust the cook time in fifteen minutes increments.

☼ Then, press the start/stop button to start cooking.

☼ When the cooking time reaches zero, the cooking appliance will beep, and the display screen will show "END." The cooking appliance automatically turns to KEEP WARM cooking mode at the end of each cooking function.

Bake

☼ To turn on the unit: Press the power button.

☼ Add ingredients into the pot according to the recipe instructions.

☼ Use the dial button and select the cooking mode "BAKE."

☼ The default temperature will show onto the screen. Use the +/- temperature arrow to adjust the temperature between 250 degrees Fahrenheit to 425 degrees Fahrenheit. You can select the temperature according to the recipe instructions.

☼ The cooking time will default to three hours. Use the +/- cooking time arrow to adjust the cooking time in one minute increment up to 1 hour or five minutes increments up to six hours. You can select the cooking time according to the recipe instructions.

☼ Then, press the start/stop button to start cooking.

☼ When the cooking time reaches zero, the cooking appliance will beep, and the display screen will show "END" for five minutes. If your food needs more time, press the plus or minus button to add more time. The cooking appliance automatically turns to KEEP WARM cooking mode at the end of each cooking function.

Proof

☼ To turn on the unit: Press the power button.

☼ Add the dough in the pot and place the cooking lid on the top.

☼ Use the dial button and select the cooking mode "PROOF."

☼ The default temperature will show onto the screen. The default temperature will show onto the screen. Use the +/- temperature arrow to adjust the temperature in five degrees increment between 90 degrees Fahrenheit to 105 degrees Fahrenheit. You can select the temperature according to the recipe instructions.

☼ Press +/- cooking time arrow to adjust the cooking time in five minute increment. You can select the cooking time according to the recipe instructions.

☼ Then, press the start/stop button to start cooking.

☼ When the cooking time reaches zero, the cooking appliance will beep, and "END" will flash three times onto the display screen. The cooking appliance automatically turns to KEEP WARM cooking mode at the end of each cooking function.

NOTE: When you poke the dough with your finger, the indentation will hold its shape and disappear slowly. If it needs more time to proof, the dough will spring back and not hold the indentation.

Instructions for Your Protection

☼ Don't allow your children to play with the appliance. It can be dangerous for them. Please keep it away from your children.

☼ Don't immerse the cord and plug in the water or any liquid to protect it from electrical shock.

☼ Don't put your appliance near the heating element like a stovetop or preheated oven.

☼ Don't immerse the main unit in the water or any liquid. It will damage your unit.

☼ Don't use the unit without the cooking pot.

☼ Before putting the removable cooking pot into the unit, ensure the cooking base is dry and clean. Otherwise, clean it with a damp cloth and then place the removable cooking pot.

☼ Without adding ingredients, don't heat the unit for more than 10 minutes. Otherwise, it will damage the cooking surface.

☼ Don't use this unit for deep frying.

☼ Don't add frozen ingredients to the pot.

☼ Touch the unit carefully while cooking food because it is very hot to touch. It will damage your skin.

☼ You can use this appliance only at home or in restaurants. Please don't use it in moving vehicles or boats. Moreover, don't use it outside. Otherwise, it will cause injury.

☼ Regularly check the power cord and appliance before starting cooking. If the unit is damaged in any way, stop using it and call customer service.

☼ Assemble the unit properly before using it.

☼ When the cooking process is done, don't place the hot pot on an unprotected surface. Always put the hot pot onto the rack or trivet. Otherwise, it will damage the surface.

☼ Hold the cooking lid with a soft cloth while cooking because it is very hot to the touch.

- ☼ Don't overfill the cooking pot with ingredients. It may cause injury or damage to the unit.
- ☼ Don't touch accessories during or immediately after cooking, as they become extremely hot during the cooking process. Use long-handled utensils and hot pads or oven mitts.
- ☼ Use a thermometer to check the tenderness of the food.
- ☼ Don't lift or move the appliance while using it.
- ☼ Put the appliance away from walls or cabinets while in use.
- ☼ This unit is used for cooking instant rice.
- ☼ Place the lid on the pot when using the "slow cook" cooking mode.
- ☼ The inner pot is oven safe up to 500 degrees Fahrenheit.
- ☼ Use the Keep Warm mode to keep food at a warm, food-safe temperature after cooking.

- The preheating time is depending onto the quantity and temperature of the ingredients.
- Use handles to lift out the pot.
- Extra food can be stored into the air-tight containers or freeze-friendly containers.
- Don't use abrasive chemicals to clean the parts of the pot.
- When the pot gets dry, place the parts back into the pot.
- Allow the unit to cook before cleaning.

Cleaning and Maintenance Process of Ninja Foodi PossibleCooker PRO

The unit must be cleaned completely after every use. It will protect your equipment and run for a long time.

- First, unplug the unit from the wall outlet and ensure that the unit is cooled before washing.
- When the unit is cooled, clean the control panel and cooker base with a clean damp cloth. Please don't put the main unit into the dishwasher, or don't immerse it in any liquid.
- If any food residue is stuck into the cooking pot, crisper tray, and bake accessory, fill it with water and allow it to soak before cleaning.
- Don't use harsh or scouring pads to remove the stuck food. Always use a non-abrasive cleanser or liquid dish soap with a nylon pad or brush.
- The spoon ladle and glass lid can be rinsed into the dishwasher. If there is any residue stuck onto the glass lid or spoon ladle, use a non-abrasive cleanser.
- When all parts get dry, return them to the unit.

Troubleshooting

1. The unit is not turned on.

Ensure that the appliance is plugged into the outlet. If not, try another outlet and plug in it. Reset the circuit breaker if needed.

2. The display shows "ADD POT" on the screen.

The cooking pot is not inside the unit. Open the lid and reset the cooking pot.

3. The display shows "ADD WATER" on the screen.

There is less water in the pot. Add more water to the unit to continue the cooking cycle.

4. The display shows a slow counting time on the screen.

You set the time in hours, not in minutes. When adjusting the cooking time, the display will show HH: MM on the screen, and time will increase or decrease in the minute increment.

5. The unit is counting up rather than down.

The cooking time is completed, and now the unit is in KEEP WARM mode.

6. Why is the unit shut off?

If you do not choose the cooking function within ten minutes, the unit will turn off automatically.

Temperature Charts

Steam chart:

Vegetable	Water	Preparation	Seasoning ideas	Steam time
Zucchini	One cup	One inch slices	Olive oil and Italian seasoning	5 to 8 minutes
Swiss chard	One cup	Chopped	Garlic and olive oil	3 to 5 minutes
Turnip greens	One cup	Chopped	Garlic and olive oil	4 to 8 minutes
Turnip	One cup	½ inch slices	Italian seasoning, garlic, ginger	8 to 12 minutes

Butternut squash	One cup	Peeled, ½ inch slices	Maple syrup	7 to 10 minutes
Spinach	One cup	Whole leaves	Garlic and olive oil	3 to 5 minutes
Sweet potato	One cup	½ inch slices	Honey or maple syrup	8 to 12 minutes
New potatoes	Four cups	Whole	Rosemary or parsley, garlic	15 to 20 minutes
All types of potatoes	One cup	½ inch slices	Dill, parsley, black pepper	8 to 12 minutes
Sugar snap, peas	One cup	Trimmed, whole pods	Lemon or lime juice, mint, parsley	5 to 6 minutes
Green peas	One cup	Fresh or frozen, shelled	Lime or lime juice, mint, ginger	2 to 4 minutes
Parsnips	One cup	Peeled, ½ inch slices	Garlic and Italian seasoning	7 to 10 minutes
Pearl onion	One cup	Whole	Lemon or lime juice, garlic	8 to 12 minutes
Okra	One cup	Trimmed, whole	Chilies and sautéed scallions or onion	6 to 8 minutes
Kale	One cup	Trimmed	Garlic, olive oil, and parsley	5 to 8 minutes
Corn on the cob	Two cups	Whole, husks discard	Black pepper, garlic butter	15 to 20 minutes
Cauliflower	One cup	Cut into florets	Lemon or lime juice, garlic, chilies	5 to 10 minutes
Baby carrot	One cup	Whole	Maple syrup or honey and ginger	7 to 10 minutes
Carrots	One cup	¼ inch slices	Maple syrup or honey	7 to 10 minutes

Cabbage	One cup	Cut into wedges	Lemon or lime juice, sautéed onion	6 to 10 minutes
Brussels sprouts	One cup	Trimmed, whole	Thyme, dill, and parsley	8 to 15 minutes
Broccoli	One cup	Florets	Olive oil, black pepper, and salt	5 to 7 minutes
Broccoli	One cup	Trimmed stalks	Olive oil, sautéed onion, and black pepper	1 to 5 minutes
Beet greens	One cup	Chopped	Parsley and thyme	7 to 9 minutes
Beets	Four cups	Chopped	Ginger, minced garlic, and sea salt	35 to 50 minutes
Wax beans	One cup	Whole	Olive oil or sunflower oil and Italian seasoning	6 to 10 minutes
Green beans	One cup	Whole	Minced garlic, ginger, and olive oil	6 to 10 minutes
Asparagus	One cup	Whole spears	Olive oil, black pepper, and sautéed onion	7 to 13 minutes
Artichoke	Four cups	Whole	Lemon or lime zest, olive oil or sunflower oil	25 to 40 minutes

Slow cook chart:

Type of Meat	Cook time LO	Cook time HI
Beef:		
Meatballs, frozen, pre-cooked	6 to 8 hours	3 to 4 hours
Top or bottom round	8 to 10 hours	4 to 5 hours

Chunk	8 to 10 hours	4 to 5 hours
Short ribs	7 to 9 hours	3 ½ to 4 ½ hours
Eye of the round	6 to 8 hours	3 to 4 hours
Brisket or Pot roast	7 to 9 hours	3 ½ to 4 ½ hours
Pork:		
Ham, pre-cooked	5 to 7 hours	2 ½ to 3 ½ hours
Baby back or country ribs	7 to 9 hours	3 ½ to 4 ½ hours
Pork butt or rib roast	7 to 9 hours	3 ½ to 4 ½ hours
Ham, bone-in, uncooked	7 to 9 hours	3 ½ to 4 ½ hours
Pork butt or pork shoulder	10 to 12 hours	5 to 6 hours
Pork tenderloin	6 to 7 hours	3 to 4 hours
Poultry		
Turkey breast or thighs	7 to 9 hours	3 ½ to 4 ½ hours
Chicken breast, skinless, boneless	6 to 7 hours	3 to 4 hours
Chicken wings	6 to 7 hours	3 to 4 hours
Chicken thighs or bone-in	6 to 7 ½ hours	3 ½ to 4 ½ hours
Chicken thighs, skinless, boneless	6 to 7 ½ hours	3 to 4 ½ hours
Whole chicken	7 to 9 hours	3 ½ to 4 ½ hours
Fish:		
1-inch fish fillets	N/A	30 to 45 minutes
Others:		
Stew meat (rabbit, veal, beef, and lamb)	7 to 9 hours	3 to 4 hours

Sous vide:

Beef	Temperature	Cook time
Ribeye, boneless	125 degrees Fahrenheit, rare	1 to 5 hours
Beef brisket	145 degrees Fahrenheit	24 to 48 hours
Pork:		
Pork chops, boneless	145 degrees Fahrenheit	1 to 4 hours
Pork tenderloin	145 degrees Fahrenheit	1 to 4 hours
Chicken:		
Chicken breast	165 degrees Fahrenheit	1 to 3 hours
Chicken thighs, boneless	165 degrees Fahrenheit	1 to 3 hours
Chicken thighs, bone-in	165 degrees Fahrenheit	1 to 3 hours
Seafood:		
White fish (haddock, cod)	130 degrees Fahrenheit	1 hour to 1 ½ hours
Salmon	130 degrees Fahrenheit	1 hour to 1 ½ hours
Shrimp	130 degrees Fahrenheit	30 minutes to 2 hours
Vegetable:		
Cauliflower	180 degrees Fahrenheit	30 minutes
Asparagus	180 degrees Fahrenheit	30 minutes
Broccoli	180 degrees Fahrenheit	30 minutes
Green beans	180 degrees Fahrenheit	30 minutes
Carrots	180 degrees Fahrenheit	45 minutes

4-Week Meal Plan

Week 1

Day 1:
Breakfast: Cherry & Pumpkin Seed Granola
Lunch: Mashed Potatoes
Dinner: Lemon & Garlicky Chicken Thighs
Dessert: Aromatic Cinnamon Pecans

Day 2:
Breakfast: Blueberry Millet Porridge
Lunch: Cheesy Colorful Vegetables Casserole
Dinner: Spicy Pork Ragù
Dessert: Crunchy Coconut Cacao Oats Cookies

Day 3:
Breakfast: Carrot, Fennel and Quinoa Casserole
Lunch: Balsamic Summer Vegetables
Dinner: Turkey and Sweet Potato Chili
Dessert: Tropical Coconut-Vanilla Yogurt

Day 4:
Breakfast: Healthy Caramel-Apple Oats
Lunch: Tikka Masala
Dinner: Juicy Pulled Pork Tacos
Dessert: Salted Drinking Chocolate

Day 5:
Breakfast: Steel-Cut Oats
Lunch: Balsamic Garlic Onions
Dinner: Beef Roast and Sweet Potatoes
Dessert: Tangy Cran-Apple Pear Compote

Day 6:
Breakfast: Spinach and Feta Quiche
Lunch: Spicy Garlicky Kale and Tomatoes
Dinner: Spicy Chili-Lime Pork Tenderloins
Dessert: Cranberry-Pineapple Punch

Day 7:
Breakfast: Creamy Vanilla-Maple Farina
Lunch: Cheesy Garlicky Smashed Potatoes
Dinner: Garlicky Parmesan Chicken
Dessert: Cranberries and Pistachios Stuffed Apples

Week 2

Day 1:
Breakfast: Strawberry-Banana Quinoa
Lunch: Garlicky Pinto Beans
Dinner: Beef Roast and Sweet Potatoes
Dessert: Lemony Cinnamon Apples and Pears

Day 2:
Breakfast: Berry Oatmeal
Lunch: Herbed Orange Cauliflower
Dinner: Five-Spice Wings
Dessert: Vanilla Tapioca Pudding

Day 3:
Breakfast: Cranberry-Quinoa Cereal
Lunch: Cheese Mushroom Risotto
Dinner: Beef & Mushroom Noodles
Dessert: Nutty Apples

Day 4:
Breakfast: Healthy Mediterranean Strata
Lunch: Cheese Barley with Root Vegetable
Dinner: Lemon-Garlicky Pork Chops
Dessert: Carrot Pudding

Day 5:
Breakfast: Berry Nuts Granola
Lunch: Thai-style Vegetables Stew
Dinner: Spicy BBQ Chicken
Dessert: Chocolate-Nut Clusters

Day 6:
Breakfast: Potato & Egg Strata
Lunch: Buttery Creamy Corn
Dinner: Turkey Meatballs
Dessert: Aromatic Cinnamon Pecans

Day 7:
Breakfast: Fruit and Nuts Oatmeal
Lunch: Eggplant in Tomato Sauce with Pasta
Dinner: Beef & Pork Chili
Dessert: Crunchy Coconut Cacao Oats Cookies

Week 3

Day 1:
Breakfast: Carrot, Fennel and Quinoa Casserole
Lunch: Beans and Green Chiles Soup
Dinner: Rotisserie Whole Chicken
Dessert: Tropical Coconut-Vanilla Yogurt

Day 2:
Breakfast: Healthy Caramel-Apple Oats
Lunch: Quinoa and Beans Bowl
Dinner: Herbed Balsamic Lamb Chops
Dessert: Salted Drinking Chocolate

Day 3:
Breakfast: Blueberry Millet Porridge
Lunch: Black Beans Soup
Dinner: Delicious Turkey Sloppy Joes
Dessert: Tangy Cran-Apple Pear Compote

Day 4:
Breakfast: Cherry & Pumpkin Seed Granola
Lunch: Cheesy Green Bean Casserole
Dinner: Roast Pork and Cabbage
Dessert: Cranberry-Pineapple Punch

Day 5:
Breakfast: Spinach and Feta Quiche
Lunch: Creamy Chickpea and Veggie Gumbo
Dinner: Beef and Barley Stew
Dessert: Cranberries and Pistachios Stuffed Apples

Day 6:
Breakfast: Creamy Vanilla-Maple Farina
Lunch: Spanish Rice & Black Beans Stuffed Peppers
Dinner: Buttery Chicken with Cheese Baguette
Dessert: Lemony Cinnamon Apples and Pears

Day 7:
Breakfast: Steel-Cut Oats
Lunch: Tangy Coconut Jackfruit with Chickpeas
Dinner: Tangy Honey Mustard Pork Roast
Dessert: Vanilla Tapioca Pudding

Week 4

Day 1:
Breakfast: Fruit and Nuts Oatmeal
Lunch: Cheesy Wheat Berry and Cranberry Pilaf
Dinner: Maple-Balsamic Lamb Stew
Dessert: Nutty Apples

Day 2:
Breakfast: Potato & Egg Strata
Lunch: Red Kidney Beans with Rice
Dinner: Delicious Miso Chicken
Dessert: Carrot Pudding

Day 3:
Breakfast: Berry Nuts Granola
Lunch: Sweet Beans Casserole
Dinner: Curried Pork Chops
Dessert: Chocolate-Nut Clusters

Day 4:
Breakfast: Healthy Mediterranean Strata
Lunch: Mushroom and Peas Risotto
Dinner: Beef & Potato Stew
Dessert: Aromatic Cinnamon Pecans

Day 5:
Breakfast: Cranberry-Quinoa Cereal
Lunch: Barley and Mushroom Risotto
Dinner: Indian Coconut Chicken and Rice
Dessert: Tropical Coconut-Vanilla Yogurt

Day 6:
Breakfast: Berry Oatmeal
Lunch: Mashed Potatoes
Dinner: Turkey and Vegetables Chili
Dessert: Salted Drinking Chocolate

Day 7:
Breakfast: Strawberry-Banana Quinoa
Lunch: Balsamic Summer Vegetables
Dinner: Beef Roast with Mushroom & Carrot
Dessert: Tangy Cran-Apple Pear Compote

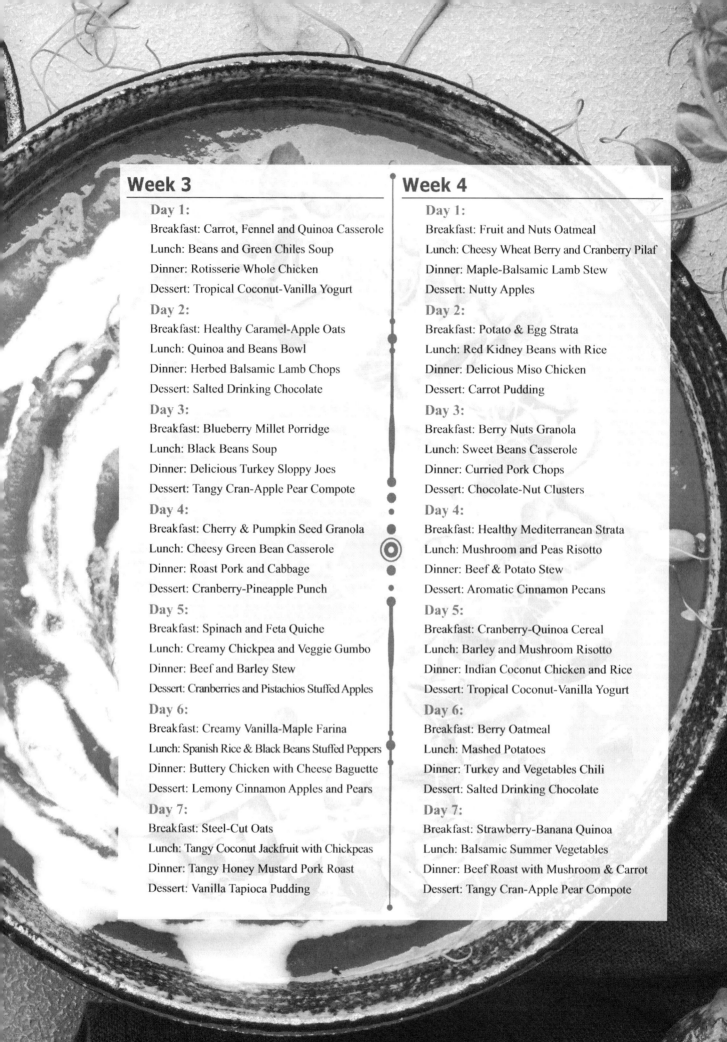

Berry Nuts Granola

Prep time: 15 minutes | Cook time: 3½ to 5 hours | Serves: 20

10 cups rolled oats

2 cups whole almonds

2 cups whole walnuts

2 cups macadamia nuts

½ cup honey

2 teaspoons ground cinnamon

¼ teaspoon ground cardamom

1 tablespoon vanilla extract

2 cups dried blueberries

2 cups dried cherries

1. In a slow cooker, mix the oatmeal, almonds, walnuts, and macadamia nuts. 2. In a bowl, mix the honey, cinnamon, cardamom, and vanilla. Drizzle this mixture over the oatmeal mixture in the slow cooker and stir with a spatula to coat. 3. Cover the slow cooker. Cook on low temp setting for 3½ to 5 hours, stirring twice during cooking time, until the oatmeal and nuts are toasted. 4. Remove the granola from the slow cooker and spread on two baking sheets. Add the dried blueberries and cherries to the granola and stir gently. 5. Let the granola cool, then store in an airtight container at room temperature up to one week.

Per Serving: Calories 649; Fat 55.2g; Sodium 1336mg; Carbs 15.2g; Fiber 9.2g; Sugar 2.1g; Protein 21.3g

Blueberry Millet Porridge

Prep time: 15 minutes | Cook time: 7 to 8 hours | Serves: 4

1 cup millet

2 cups water

2 cups full-fat coconut milk

½ teaspoon sea salt

½ teaspoon ground cinnamon

½ teaspoon ground ginger

¼ teaspoon vanilla extract

½ cup fresh blueberries

1. In slow cooker, combine the millet, water, coconut milk, salt, cinnamon, ginger, and vanilla. Stir well. 2. Cover the slow cooker and set to low temp setting. Cook for 7 to 8 hours. 3. Stir in the blueberries to warm at the end and serve.

Per Serving: Calories 288; Fat 26g; Sodium 311mg; Carbs 10g; Fiber 2g; Sugar 7g; Protein 3g

Carrot, Fennel and Quinoa Casserole

Prep time: 15 minutes | Cook time: 5 to 7 hours | Serves: 4 to 6

6 eggs

½ cup quinoa, rinsed well

1½ cups unsweetened almond milk

½ teaspoon sea salt

½ teaspoon garlic powder

¼ teaspoon dried oregano

Freshly ground black pepper

1 fennel bulb, finely sliced

3 medium carrots, diced

1 tablespoon extra-virgin olive oil

1. In a bowl, whisk the eggs. 2. Add the quinoa, almond milk, salt, garlic powder, and oregano, and spice with pepper. Whisk until all ingredients are combined. 3. Stir in the fennel and carrots. 4. Grease the slow cooker with the olive oil, and slowly pour in the egg mixture. 5. Cover the slow cooker and set to low temp setting. Cook for 5 to 7 hours and serve.

Per Serving: Calories 336; Fat 32g; Sodium 313mg; Carbs 11g; Fiber 3g; Sugar 4g; Protein 3g

Healthy Caramel–Apple Oats

Prep time: 15 minutes | Cook time: 6 to 8 hours | Serves: 4

1 tablespoon coconut oil

3 sweet apples, such as Fuji or Gala, peeled and sliced

2 tablespoons coconut sugar

¼ teaspoon sea salt

1 teaspoon ground ginger

1 teaspoon ground cinnamon

1 teaspoon vanilla extract

2 cups rolled oats

1 cup unsweetened applesauce

3 cups unsweetened almond milk

½ cup water

1. Grease the slow cooker with the coconut oil. 2. Layer the sliced apples in the slow cooker so each piece is touching the bottom. 3. In this order, layer in the coconut sugar, salt, ginger, cinnamon, vanilla, oats, applesauce, almond milk, and water. 4. Cover the slow cooker and set to low temp setting. Cook for 6 to 8 hours and serve.

Per Serving: Calories 336; Fat 34g; Sodium 314mg; Carbs 6g; Fiber 3g; Sugar 1g; Protein 5g

Steel–Cut Oats

Prep time: 15 minutes | Cook time: 6 to 8 hours | Serves: 4 to 6

1 tablespoon coconut oil

4 cups boiling water

½ teaspoon sea salt

1 cup steel-cut oats

1. Grease the slow cooker with the coconut oil. 2. In slow cooker, combine the boiling water, salt, and oats. 3. Cover the slow cooker and set to low temp setting. Cook for 6 to 8 hours and serve.

Per Serving: Calories 280; Fat 24g; Sodium 313mg; Carbs 14g; Fiber 4g; Sugar 6g; Protein 4g

Spinach and Feta Quiche

Prep time: 15 minutes | Cook time: 5 to 6 hours | Serves: 6

1 tablespoon extra-virgin olive oil

12 eggs

1 cup whole-grain biscuit mix or whole-grain pancake and waffle mix

1 cup 2 percent milk

2 cups baby spinach

1½ cups crumbled feta cheese, plus more for topping

1 teaspoon garlic powder

½ teaspoon sea salt

1. Grease the bottom of a slow cooker with the olive oil. 2. Add the eggs, biscuit mix, and milk. Whisk until smooth. 3. Add the spinach, cheese, garlic powder, and salt. Mix well. Cover the slow cooker and cook on low temp setting for 5 to 6 hours, until the center of the quiche has set and the edges are golden brown. 4. Serve the quiche with cheese on top, if desired.

Per Serving: Calories 323; Fat 34g; Sodium 314mg; Carbs 6g; Fiber 3g; Sugar 0g; Protein 5g

Creamy Vanilla–Maple Farina

Prep time: 5 minutes | Cook time: 8 hours | Serves: 4

¾ cup cream of wheat

½ teaspoon sea salt

2 cups water

2 cups 2 percent milk

¾ teaspoon vanilla extract

¼ cup pure maple syrup, plus more for topping

1. In a slow cooker, combine the cream of wheat, salt, water, milk, vanilla, and maple syrup. Cover the slow cooker and cook on low temp setting for 8 hours, until thick and creamy. 2. Serve the farina warm, topped with maple syrup.

Per Serving: Calories 334; Fat 34g; Sodium 314mg; Carbs 6g; Fiber 3g; Sugar 1g; Protein 5g

Prep time: 10 minutes | Cook time: 6 to 8 hours | Serves: 6

1½ cups quinoa, rinsed

3 cups unsweetened cashew, coconut, or flax milk

2 cups fresh strawberries, halved, plus for more topping

1 banana, peeled and sliced, plus more for topping

3 tablespoons almond butter or peanut butter

1. In a slow cooker, mix the quinoa, milk, strawberries, banana, and nut butter. Cover the slow cooker and cook on low temp setting for 6 to 8 hours, until the liquid has been absorbed. 2. Serve the quinoa warm, topped with berries or banana.

Per Serving: Calories 90; Fat 6.5g; Sodium 186mg; Carbs 0.6g; Fiber 0g; Sugar 0.3g; Protein 5.8g

Prep time: 20 minutes | Cook time: 8 to 10 hours | Serves: 12

10 yellow onions, peeled and sliced

20 garlic cloves, peeled

¼ cup olive oil

¼ teaspoon salt

2 tablespoons balsamic vinegar

1 teaspoon dried thyme leaves

1. In a slow cooker, mix all of the ingredients. Cover the slow cooker and cook on low temp setting for 8 to 10 hours, stirring twice.

Per Serving: Calories 350; Fat 29g; Sodium 621mg; Carbs 10g; Fiber 4g; Sugar 3g; Protein 14g

Cranberry–Quinoa Cereal

Prep time: 15 minutes | Cook time: 6 to 8 hours | Serves: 12

3 cups quinoa, rinsed and drained

2 cups unsweetened apple juice

4 cups canned coconut milk

2 cups water

¼ cup honey

1 teaspoon vanilla extract

1 teaspoon ground cinnamon

½ teaspoon salt

1½ cups dried cranberries

1. In a slow cooker, mix all of the ingredients. 2. Cover the slow cooker and cook on low temp setting for 6 to 8 hours or until the quinoa is creamy.

Per Serving: Calories 620; Fat 49.6g; Sodium 1746mg; Carbs 4.7g; Fiber 1.2g; Sugar 1.7g; Protein 29.8g

Berry Oatmeal

Prep time: 15 minutes | Cook time: 4 to 6 hours | Serves: 12

7 cups rolled oats

4 eggs

1½ cups almond milk

2 tablespoons melted coconut oil

⅓ cup honey

¼ teaspoon salt

1 teaspoon ground cinnamon

¼ teaspoon ground ginger

1½ cups dried blueberries

1 cup dried cherries

1. Grease a slow cooker with vegetable oil. 2. In a bowl, place the rolled oats. 3. In a bowl, mix the eggs, almond milk, coconut oil, honey, salt, cinnamon, and ginger. Mix until well combined. Pour this mixture over the oats. 4. Gently stir in the dried blueberries and dried cherries. Pour into the prepared slow cooker. 5. Cover the slow cooker and cook on low temp setting for 4 to 6 hours until the oatmeal mixture is set and the edges start to brown.

Per Serving: Calories 201; Fat 14g; Sodium 1314mg; Carbs 3.1g; Fiber 0.6g; Sugar 1.6g; Protein 13.3g

Fruit and Nuts Oatmeal

Prep time: 20 minutes | Cook time: 5 to 7 hours | Serves: 1

2 cups whole or 2% milk

¼ cup brown sugar

2 tablespoon honey

2 tablespoon melted butter

¼ teaspoon salt

½ teaspoon cinnamon

1 cup steel cut or regular oats

1 cup apples, peeled, chopped

½ cup dates, raisins, chopped

½ cup nuts, chopped

1. Grease the slow cooker with cooking spray. Combine milk, brown sugar, honey, melted butter, salt, and cinnamon in the slow cooker and mix well. 2. Mix in the oats, apples, dates or raisins, and the nuts. 3. Cover the slow cooker and turn on low temp setting. Cook 5-7 hours until oatmeal is tender. Stir well before serving.

Per Serving: Calories 107; Fat 7.7g; Sodium 387mg; Carbs 0.4g; Fiber 0g; Sugar 0g; Protein 7.8g

Healthy Mediterranean Strata

Prep time: 20 minutes | Cook time: 5 to 7 hours | Serves: 10

8 cups whole-wheat bread, cut into cubes

1 onion, finely chopped

3 garlic cloves, minced

2 red bell peppers, stemmed, seeded, and chopped

2 cups chopped baby spinach leaves

4 eggs

2 egg whites

2 tablespoons olive oil

1½ cups 2% milk

1 cup shredded Asiago cheese

1. In a slow cooker, mix the bread cubes, onion, garlic, bell peppers, and spinach. 2. In a bowl, mix the eggs, egg whites, olive oil, and milk, and beat well. Pour this mixture into the slow cooker. Sprinkle with the cheese. 3. Cover the slow cooker and cook on low temp setting for 5 to 7 hours until the strata is set and puffed. 4. Scoop the strata out of the slow cooker to serve.

Per Serving: Calories 77; Fat 4.4g; Sodium 62mg; Carbs 0.6g; Fiber 0g; Sugar 0.6g; Protein 6.3g

Prep time: 10 minutes | Cook time: 5 to 6 hours | Serves: 4 to 6

5 tablespoons melted coconut oil, divided

1 cup unsweetened shredded coconut

1 cup rolled oats

1 cup pecans

½ cup pumpkin seeds

1 ripe banana

1 tablespoon vanilla extract

½ teaspoon sea salt

½ teaspoon ground cinnamon

½ teaspoon ground ginger

1 cup dried sour cherries

1. Grease the slow cooker with 1 tablespoon of coconut oil. 2. In slow cooker, toss the coconut, oats, pecans, and pumpkin seeds. 3. In a bowl, mash the banana with the remaining 4 tablespoons of melted coconut oil, the vanilla, salt, cinnamon, and ginger. 4. Add the liquid ingredients to the granola mixture and stir well to combine. 5. Cover the slow cooker and set to low temp setting. Cook for 5 to 6 hours. 6. When the cooking is finished, stir in the cherries. 7. Spread the granola on a flat surface or baking sheet to cool and dry completely before storing in airtight containers.

Per Serving: Calories 360; Fat 37g; Sodium 317mg; Carbs 7g; Fiber 3g; Sugar 1g; Protein 4g

Prep time: 20 minutes | Cook time: 6 to 8 hours | Serves: 8

8 Yukon Gold potatoes, peeled and diced

1 onion, minced

2 red bell peppers, stemmed, seeded, and minced

3 Roma tomatoes, seeded and chopped

3 garlic cloves, minced

1½ cups shredded Swiss cheese

8 eggs

2 egg whites

1 teaspoon dried marjoram leaves

1 cup 2% milk

1. In a slow cooker, layer the diced potatoes, onion, bell peppers, tomatoes, garlic, and cheese. 2. In a bowl, mix the eggs, egg whites, marjoram, and milk well with a wire whisk. Pour this mixture into the slow cooker. 3. Cover the slow cooker and cook on low temp setting for 6 to 8 hours until potatoes are tender. 4. Scoop out of the slow cooker to serve.

Per Serving: Calories 71; Fat 4.3g; Sodium 62mg; Carbs 0.4g; Fiber 0g; Sugar 0.2g; Protein 6.3g

Cheesy Colorful Vegetables Casserole

Prep time: 10 minutes | Cook time: 4 to 5 hours | Serves: 8 to 10

3 cups fresh broccoli florets

3 cups fresh cauliflower florets

2 cups baby carrots

1 (8-ounce) container plain 2 percent Greek yogurt

1½ cups shredded sharp Cheddar cheese, divided

1 cup shredded mozzarella cheese,

shredded provolone cheese, or a mix of both

1 cup 2 percent milk

1 tablespoon minced garlic

1 tablespoon minced onion

Sea salt

Ground black pepper

1. In a slow cooker, combine the broccoli, cauliflower, and carrots. 2. In a bowl, whisk the yogurt, ¾ cup of Cheddar cheese, the mozzarella cheese, milk, garlic, and onion. 3. Pour the yogurt mixture over the vegetables and mix well. Cover the slow cooker and cook on low temp setting for 4 to 5 hours, until the vegetables are soft. 4. Remove the lid and sprinkle the remaining ¾ cup of Cheddar cheese over the top. Replace the lid and cook for 5 to 10 minutes, until the cheese has melted. 5. Season with salt and black pepper. Serve the vegetables warm.

Per Serving: Calories 412; Fat 38g; Sodium 770mg; Carbs 4g; Fiber 0.5g; Sugar 0.6g; Protein 15g

Balsamic Summer Vegetables

Prep time: 15 minutes | Cook time: 4 to 5 hours | Serves: 6 to 8

½ cup extra-virgin olive oil

½ cup balsamic vinegar

2 tablespoons chopped fresh basil leaves

1 tablespoon dried thyme

1 (16-ounce) can chopped or diced tomatoes, drained

1 cup chopped white onion

2½ cups sliced or chopped cored orange and yellow bell peppers

3 cups sliced peeled zucchini

1. In a slow cooker, combine the olive oil, vinegar, basil, and thyme. Cook on high, for 2 to 3 minutes, until fragrant. 2. Add the tomatoes, onion, bell peppers, and zucchini. Mix well. Cover, reduce the heat to low, and cook for 4 to 5 hours, until the vegetables are soft. 3. Serve the vegetables warm on their own or as a side dish.

Per Serving: Calories 545; Fat 50g; Sodium 972mg; Carbs 17g; Fiber 9g; Sugar 2g; Protein 14g

Herbed Orange Cauliflower

Prep time: 20 minutes | Cook time: 4 hours | Serves: 8

2 heads cauliflower, rinsed and cut into florets

2 onions, chopped

½ cup orange juice

1 teaspoon grated orange zest

1 teaspoon dried thyme leaves

½ teaspoon dried basil leaves

½ teaspoon salt

1. In a slow cooker, mix the cauliflower and onions. Top with the orange juice and orange zest, and drizzle with the thyme, basil, and salt. 2. Cover the slow cooker and cook on low temp setting for 4 hours until the cauliflower is tender.

Per Serving: Calories 328; Fat 30g; Sodium 836mg; Carbs 10g; Fiber 5g; Sugar 2g; Protein 8g

Mashed Potatoes

Prep time: 10 minutes | Cook time: 2 to 3 hours | Serves: 8 to 10

Nonstick cooking spray, for coating the slow cooker

1¾ cups 2 percent milk

3½ cups water, heated in the microwave until hot to the touch

8 ounces cream cheese, cubed

8 tablespoons (1 stick) butter, at room temperature

½ cup 2 percent cottage cheese

¼ cup 2 percent plain yogurt

4 cups potato flakes

1 teaspoon sea salt

1. Grease the bottom and sides of a slow cooker with cooking spray. 2. Add the milk, water, cream cheese, butter, cottage cheese, and yogurt. Whisk until smooth. Stir in the potato flakes and salt. Cover the slow cooker and cook on low temp setting for 2 to 3 hours, until heated through. 3. Serve the potatoes warm as a side dish with favorite protein.

Per Serving: Calories 340; Fat 27g; Sodium 1109mg; Carbs 10g; Fiber 4g; Sugar 2g; Protein 16g

Buttery Creamy Corn

Prep time: 10 minutes | Cook time: 4 hours | Serves: 12

20 oz. frozen corn kernels from two 16 oz. packages

1 (8 ounce) package cream cheese

½ cup butter

½ cup milk

1 tablespoon white sugar

Salt and pepper to taste

1. In a slow cooker, combine corn, milk, cream cheese, butter, and sugar. Spice with salt and pepper. Cook on high temp setting for 2 to 4 hours.

Per Serving: Calories 58; Fat 6.6g; Sodium 468mg; Carbs 7.7g; Fiber 2.4g; Sugar 4.4g; Protein 1.5g

Spicy Garlicky Kale and Tomatoes

Prep time: 20 minutes | Cook time: 4 to 5 hours | Serves: 8

4 bunches kale, washed, stemmed, and cut into pieces

2 onions, chopped

8 garlic cloves, minced

2 jalapeño peppers, minced

4 tomatoes, seeded and chopped

1 tablespoon chili powder

½ teaspoon salt

⅛ teaspoon freshly ground black pepper

1. In a slow cooker, mix the kale, onions, garlic, jalapeño peppers, and tomatoes. 2. Sprinkle with the chili powder, salt, and pepper, and stir to mix. 3. Cover the slow cooker and cook on low temp setting for 4 to 5 hours until the kale is wilted and tender.

Per Serving: Calories 349; Fat 30g; Sodium 620mg; Carbs 14g; Fiber 6g; Sugar 2g; Protein 10g

Cheesy Garlicky Smashed Potatoes

Prep time: 20 minutes | Cook time: 5 to 6 hours | Serves: 6

3½ pounds red or creamer potatoes, rinsed

2 onions, minced

12 garlic cloves, peeled and sliced

½ cup Roasted Vegetable Broth

3 tablespoons olive oil

1 teaspoon dried thyme leaves

1 teaspoon dried dill leaves

½ teaspoon salt

⅓ cup grated Parmesan cheese

1. In a slow cooker, mix the potatoes, onions, garlic, vegetable broth, olive oil, thyme, dill, and salt. Cover the slow cooker and cook on low temp setting for 5 to 6 hours until the potatoes are tender. 2. Using a masher, mash the potatoes in the slow cooker, leaving some chunky pieces. Stir in the Parmesan cheese and serve.

Per Serving: Calories 321; Fat 28g; Sodium 608mg; Carbs 8g; Fiber 3g; Sugar 2g; Protein 12g

Cheese Mushroom Risotto

Prep time: 20 minutes | Cook time: 3 to 4 hours | Serves: 8

8 ounces button mushrooms, sliced

8 ounces cremini mushrooms, sliced

8 ounces shiitake mushrooms, stems removed and sliced

2 onions, chopped

5 garlic cloves, minced

2 cups short-grain brown rice

1 teaspoon dried marjoram leaves

6 cups Roasted Vegetable Broth

3 tablespoons unsalted butter

½ cup grated Parmesan cheese

1. In a slow cooker, mix the mushrooms, onions, garlic, rice, marjoram, and vegetable broth. 2. Cover the slow cooker and cook on low temp setting for 3 to 4 hours until the rice is tender. 3. Stir in the butter and cheese. Cover and cook on low for 20 minutes, then serve.

Per Serving: Calories 511; Fat 47g; Sodium 1253mg; Carbs 20g; Fiber 9g; Sugar 3g; Protein 10g

Cheese Barley with Root Vegetable

Prep time: 20 minutes | Cook time: 7 to 9 hours | Serves: 8

2 cups hulled barley

2 onions, chopped

5 garlic cloves, minced

3 carrots, peeled and sliced

2 sweet potatoes, peeled and cubed

4 Yukon Gold potatoes, cubed

7 cups Roasted Vegetable Broth

1 teaspoon dried tarragon leaves

½ cup grated Parmesan cheese

1. In a slow cooker, mix the barley, onions, garlic, carrots, sweet potatoes, and Yukon Gold potatoes. Add the vegetable broth and tarragon leaves. 2. Cover the slow cooker and cook on low temp setting for 7 to 9 hours until the barley is tender and the vegetables are tender too. 3. Stir in the cheese and serve.

Per Serving: Calories 564; Fat 44g; Sodium 1653mg; Carbs 14g; Fiber 4g; Sugar 3g; Protein 27g

Thai-style Vegetables Stew

Prep time: 20 minutes | Cook time: 6 to 8 hours | Serves: 8

4 carrots, peeled and cut into chunks

2 onions, peeled and sliced

6 garlic cloves, peeled and sliced

2 parsnips, peeled and sliced

2 jalapeño peppers, minced

½ cup Roasted Vegetable Broth

⅓ cup canned coconut milk

3 tablespoons lime juice

2 tablespoons grated fresh ginger root

2 teaspoons curry powder

1. In a slow cooker, mix the carrots, onions, garlic, parsnips, and jalapeño peppers. 2. In a bowl, mix the vegetable broth, coconut milk, lime juice, ginger root, and curry powder until well blended. Pour into the slow cooker. 3. Cover the slow cooker and cook on low temp setting for 6 to 8 hours until the vegetables are tender.

Per Serving: Calories 473; Fat 42g; Sodium 756mg; Carbs 14g; Fiber 3g; Sugar 2g; Protein 13g

Eggplant in Tomato Sauce with Pasta

Prep time: 15 minutes | Cook time: 4 hours | Serves: 6

1 medium eggplant, cut into small cubes

1 onion, finely chopped

2 cloves garlic, finely chopped

1 can (28 oz.) Muir Glen Organic diced tomatoes, drained

1 can (6 oz.) tomato paste

½ cup red wine or water

1 teaspoon dried oregano

½ teaspoon salt

1 package (16 oz.) rotini pasta

Shredded Parmesan cheese, if desired

1. Grease a slow cooker with cooking spray. In the slow cooker, mix all ingredients except pasta and cheese. 2. Cover and cook on low temp setting for 4 hours until eggplant is soft and sauce is thick. Cook the pasta 15 minutes beforehand. 3. Toss pasta with eggplant and tomato sauce. Garnish with cheese.

Per Serving: Calories 432; Fat 36g; Sodium 819mg; Carbs 8.4g; Fiber 1.3g; Sugar 2.5g; Protein 11.7g

Garlicky Pinto Beans

Prep time: 10 minutes | Cook time: 9 hours | Serves: 8

4 cups dried pinto beans, rinsed and drained

2 onions, minced

4 garlic cloves, minced

1 jalapeño pepper, minced

1 teaspoon dried oregano leaves

1 teaspoon salt

9 cups Roasted Vegetable Broth

⅓ cup olive oil

1. In a slow cooker, mix the beans, onions, garlic, jalapeño pepper, oregano, salt, and vegetable broth. Cover the slow cooker and cook on low temp setting for 8 hours until the beans are tender. 2. Add the olive oil. Use a potato masher to mash the beans right in the slow cooker. 3. Cover the slow cooker and cook on low temp setting for another 30 to 40 minutes, then serve. If the beans aren't thick enough, remove the cover and cook on high temp setting for 40 to 50 minutes longer, stirring occasionally.

Per Serving: Calories 625; Fat 51g; Sodium 1642mg; Carbs 27g; Fiber 9g; Sugar 3g; Protein 22g

Balsamic Garlic Onions

Prep time: 20 minutes | Cook time: 8 to 10 hours | Serves: 12

10 yellow onions, peeled and sliced

20 garlic cloves, peeled

¼ cup olive oil

¼ teaspoon salt

2 tablespoons balsamic vinegar

1 teaspoon dried thyme leaves

1. In a slow cooker, mix all of the ingredients. Cover the slow cooker and cook on low temp setting for 8 to 10 hours, stirring twice.

Per Serving: Calories 350; Fat 29g; Sodium 621mg; Carbs 10g; Fiber 4g; Sugar 3g; Protein 14g

Tikka Masala

Prep time: 15 minutes | Cook time: 8½ hours | Serves: 6

2 tablespoons olive oil

4 (15-ounce) cans chickpeas, drained and rinsed

1 yellow onion, chopped

5 teaspoons minced garlic

2 tablespoons grated fresh ginger

1 (15-ounce) can tomato sauce

2 teaspoons sea salt

½ teaspoon ground black pepper

1 teaspoon ground coriander

1 teaspoon ground turmeric

¼ teaspoon ground cinnamon

½ teaspoon cayenne pepper

2 teaspoons ground cumin

2 teaspoons paprika

1 tablespoon garam masala

1 cup full-fat canned coconut milk

2 tablespoons cornstarch

1 tablespoon lemon juice

Chopped fresh cilantro, for topping

1½ cups cooked brown or basmati rice

1. Grease the bottom of a slow cooker with the olive oil. 2. Add the chickpeas, onion, garlic, ginger, tomato sauce, salt, black pepper, coriander, turmeric, cinnamon, cayenne, cumin, paprika, and garam masala. Mix well so the chickpeas are well coated. Cover the slow cooker and cook on low temp setting for 8 hours, until the chickpeas are tender. 3. In a bowl, whisk the coconut milk and cornstarch to make a slurry. 4. Remove the slow cooker lid and stir in the slurry. Replace the lid and cook for 30 minutes, until the gravy has thickened. 5. Stir in the lemon juice, and garnish with the cilantro. 6. Serve the tikka masala over ¼ cup of rice per serving.

Per Serving: Calories 340; Fat 28g; Sodium 640mg; Carbs 23g; Fiber 9g; Sugar 2g; Protein 5g

Creamy Chickpea and Veggie Gumbo

Prep time: 15 minutes | Cook time: 6 hours | Serves: 6

2 tablespoons extra-virgin olive oil

1 medium sweet onion, finely chopped

2 celery ribs, finely chopped

2 tablespoons minced garlic

1 (10- to 12-ounce) package frozen sliced okra

1 small green bell pepper, diced

1 (14½-ounce) can no-salt-added diced tomatoes, with their juices

2 (15- to 16-ounce) cans no-salt-added chickpeas, drained and rinsed

1 cup no-salt-added vegetable broth

2 bay leaves

Kosher salt

Freshly ground black pepper

Chopped fresh parsley, for garnish

Hot sauce, for serving

1. In a slow cooker, combine the oil, onion, celery, garlic, okra, bell pepper, tomatoes with their juices, chickpeas, broth, and bay leaves. 2. Cover the slow cooker and cook on low temp setting for 6 hours, until the okra is soft and the flavors have melded. 3. Spiced with salt and pepper and spoon into serving bowls. Garnish with parsley and serve with hot sauce.

Per Serving: Calories 350; Fat 29g; Sodium 621mg; Carbs 10g; Fiber 4g; Sugar 3g; Protein 14g

Beans and Green Chiles Soup

Prep time: 15 minutes | Cook time: 6 to 8 hours | Serves: 4 to 6

2 cups dried pinto beans, soaked in water overnight, drained, and rinsed

7 cups vegetable broth

½ medium onion, minced

1 (4-ounce) can Hatch green chiles

1 tablespoon freshly squeezed lime juice

½ teaspoon ground cumin

½ teaspoon garlic powder

½ teaspoon sea salt

1. In slow cooker, combine the beans, broth, onion, chiles, lime juice, cumin, garlic powder, and salt. 2. Cover the slow cooker and set to low temp setting. Cook for 6 to 8 hours, until the beans are soft. 3. Using a blender to mash the beans to desired consistency before serving.

Per Serving: Calories 102; Fat 8g; Sodium 235mg; Carbs 5g; Fiber 1g; Sugar 1g; Protein 1g

Black Beans Soup

Prep time: 5 minutes | Cook time: 6 to 8 hours | Serves: 10 to 12

1 pound dried black beans, rinsed

⅛ teaspoon garlic powder

2 teaspoons onion powder

1 tablespoon sea salt

¼ cup extra-virgin olive oil

8 cups Savory Chicken Broth, Savory Vegetable Broth, or store-bought broth

1. In a slow cooker, combine the beans, garlic powder, onion powder, salt, and olive oil. 2. Pour the broth over the beans and spices. Cover the slow cooker and cook on low temp setting for 6 to 8 hours, until the beans are very soft and most of the liquid has been absorbed. 3. Serve the beans warm.

Per Serving: Calories 96; Fat 5g; Sodium 451mg; Carbs 6g; Fiber 1g; Sugar 1g; Protein 4g

Spanish Rice & Black Beans Stuffed Peppers

Prep time: 15 minutes | Cook time: 4 to 5 hours | Serves: 4

1 tablespoon avocado oil

4 bell peppers, any color, washed, tops cut off, and seeded

½ cup water

2 cups Spanish Rice

1 (15-ounce) can black beans, rinsed and drained well

1. Grease the bottom of the slow cooker with the avocado oil. 2. Place the peppers, upright, in the cooker. Add the water to the bottom of the slow cooker, around the outside of the peppers. 3. In a bowl, stir the rice and black beans. Stuff each pepper with one-quarter of the mixture. 4. Cover the slow cooker and set to low temp setting. Cook for 4 to 5 hours and serve.

Per Serving: Calories 349; Fat 30g; Sodium 620mg; Carbs 14g; Fiber 6g; Sugar 2g; Protein 10g

Mushroom and Peas Risotto

Prep time: 15 minutes | Cook time: 2 to 3 hours | Serves: 4 to 6

1½ cups Arborio rice

1 cup English peas

1 small shallot, minced

¼ cup dried porcini mushrooms

4½ cups broth of choice

1 tablespoon freshly squeezed lemon juice

½ teaspoon garlic powder

½ teaspoon sea salt

1. In slow cooker, combine the rice, peas, shallot, mushrooms, broth, lemon juice, garlic powder, and salt. Stir to mix well. 2. Cover the slow cooker and set to high temp setting. Cook for 2 to 3 hours and serve.

Per Serving: Calories 113; Fat 7g; Sodium 606mg; Carbs 10g; Fiber 3.2g; Sugar 8.1g; Protein 3.9g

Cheesy Wheat Berry and Cranberry Pilaf

Prep time: 20 minutes | Cook time: 8 to 10 hours | Serves: 10

3 cups wheat berries, rinsed and drained

2 leeks, peeled, rinsed, and chopped

7 cups Roasted Vegetable Broth

2 tablespoons lemon juice

1½ cups dried cranberries

1 teaspoon dried thyme leaves

¼ teaspoon salt

1 cup chopped pecans

1½ cups shredded baby Swiss cheese

1. In a slow cooker, mix the wheat berries, leeks, vegetable broth, lemon juice, cranberries, thyme, and salt. 2. Cover the slow cooker and cook on low temp setting for 8 to 10 hours until the wheat berries are tender, but still slightly chewy. 3. Add the pecans and cheese. Cover and let stand for 10 minutes, then serve.

Per Serving: Calories 625; Fat 51g; Sodium 1642mg; Carbs 27g; Fiber 9g; Sugar 3g; Protein 22g

Barley and Mushroom Risotto

Prep time: 15 minutes | Cook time: 7 to 8 hours | Serves: 8

2¼ cups hulled barley, rinsed

1 onion, finely chopped

4 garlic cloves, minced

1 (8-ounce) package button mushrooms, chopped

6 cups low-sodium vegetable broth

½ teaspoon dried marjoram leaves

⅛ teaspoon freshly ground black pepper

⅔ cup grated Parmesan cheese

1. In a slow cooker, mix the barley, onion, garlic, mushrooms, broth, marjoram, and pepper. Cover the slow cooker and cook on low temp setting for 7 to 8 hours until the barley has absorbed most of the liquid and is tender, and the vegetables are tender. 2. Stir in the Parmesan cheese and serve.

Per Serving: Calories 123; Fat 10.9g; Sodium 601mg; Carbs 4.3g; Fiber 0.1g; Sugar 0g; Protein 2.4g

Prep time: 10 minutes | Cook time: 3 hours | Serves: 4

1 cup quinoa, rinsed and drained

1½ cups water

1 (10-ounce) can diced tomatoes with green chiles

1 (15-ounce) can black beans, rinsed and drained

2 tablespoons fresh lime juice

1 teaspoon garlic powder

½ teaspoon salt

Freshly ground black pepper

1 avocado, peeled, pitted, and sliced

1. Combine the quinoa, water, diced tomatoes with their juices, black beans, lime juice, garlic powder, and salt in the slow cooker. 2. Cover the slow cooker and cook on low temp setting for 3 hours. Remove the lid and fluff the ingredients with a fork. Season with salt and pepper, if needed. 3. Scoop the quinoa and vegetables into serving bowls. Top each portion with avocado slices and serve.

Per Serving: Calories 349; Fat 1g; Sodium 236mg; Carbs 4g; Fiber 1g; Sugar 2g; Protein 0g

Tangy Coconut Jackfruit with Chickpeas

Prep time: 15 minutes | Cook time: 6 to 8 hours | Serves: 4

1 (20-ounce) can young jackfruit in water, drained

1 (15-ounce) can chickpeas, rinsed and drained

1 (15-ounce) can diced tomatoes, with their juice

1 (15-ounce) can full-fat coconut milk or coconut cream

1 cup low-sodium vegetable broth

1 onion, diced

3 garlic cloves, minced

Handful fresh cilantro leaves

2 teaspoons curry powder

1½ teaspoons ground ginger

1 teaspoon ground coriander

½ teaspoon ground turmeric

½ teaspoon salt

1. Combine all the ingredients in the slow cooker and mix well. 2. Cover the slow cooker and cook on low temp setting for 6 to 8 hours.

Per Serving: Calories 321; Fat 28g; Sodium 608mg; Carbs 8g; Fiber 3g; Sugar 2g; Protein 12g

Red Kidney Beans with Rice

Prep time: 15 minutes | Cook time: 8 hours | Serves: 6 to 8

1 (14- to 16-ounce) can red kidney beans, drained and rinsed

4 cups Savory Chicken Broth or store-bought chicken broth

6 cups water

1-pound andouille, chorizo, smoked beef sausage, or ham, sliced

1 medium yellow onion, chopped

1 orange or yellow bell pepper, cored and chopped

1 cup chopped celery

¼ cup minced garlic

1 teaspoon ground black pepper

2 tablespoons Creole Seasoning

6 to 8 cups cooked brown or wild rice

1. Put the beans in the bottom of a slow cooker, then pour the broth and water over the beans. 2. Add the sausage, onion, bell pepper, celery, garlic, black pepper, and Creole Seasoning. Mix well. Cover the slow cooker and cook on low temp setting for 8 hours, until the beans are soft and easily mashed. 3. Serve the beans warm over the rice.

Per Serving: Calories 511; Fat 47g; Sodium 1253mg; Carbs 20g; Fiber 9g; Sugar 3g; Protein 10g

Sweet Beans Casserole

Prep time: 15 minutes | Cook time: 8 hours | Serves: 4

1 (15-ounce) can pinto beans, rinsed and drained

1 (15-ounce) can kidney beans, rinsed and drained

1 (15-ounce) can great northern beans, rinsed and drained

2 red or green bell peppers, seeded and diced

2 tomatoes, diced

1 onion, diced

3 garlic cloves, minced

¼ cup yellow or Dijon mustard

¼ cup honey or maple syrup

2 teaspoons salt

1 teaspoon freshly ground black pepper

1 teaspoon ground cumin

½ teaspoon chili powder

1. Combine all the ingredients in the slow cooker and mix well. 2. Cover the slow cooker and cook on low temp setting for 8 hours.

Per Serving: Calories 473; Fat 42g; Sodium 756mg; Carbs 14g; Fiber 3g; Sugar 2g; Protein 13g

Prep time: 15 minutes | Cook time: 6 hours | Serves: 6

¼ cup butter, divided

½ sweet onion, chopped

1 cup sliced button mushrooms

1 teaspoon minced garlic

2 pounds green beans, cut into 2-inch pieces

1 cup chicken broth

8 ounces cream cheese

¼ cup grated parmesan cheese

1. Lightly grease the slow cooker with 1 tablespoon of the butter. 2. In a skillet over medium-high heat, melt the remaining butter. add the onion, mushrooms, and garlic and sauté for about 5 minutes until the vegetables are softened. 3. Stir the green beans into the skillet and transfer the mixture to the insert. 4. In a bowl, whisk the broth and cream cheese until smooth. 5. Add the cheese mixture to the vegetables and stir. Top the combined mixture with the parmesan. 6. Cover the slow cooker and cook on low temp setting for 6 hours. 7. Serve warm.

Per Serving: Calories 340; Fat 27g; Sodium 1109mg; Carbs 10g; Fiber 4g; Sugar 2g; Protein 16g

Turkey and Vegetables Chili

Prep time: 15 minutes | Cook time: 7-8 hours | Serves: 6-8

3 tablespoons extra-virgin olive oil

1 tablespoon minced garlic

1 white onion, chopped

3 pounds ground turkey

1 red bell pepper, cored and chopped

1 yellow bell pepper, cored and chopped

1 orange bell pepper, cored and chopped

1 sweet potato, peeled and chopped

1 zucchini, peeled and chopped

1 to 1½ cups water

2 teaspoons sea salt

½ teaspoon ground black pepper

3 tablespoons low-sodium soy sauce or coconut aminos

1 tablespoon dried oregano

2 teaspoons paprika

2 teaspoons chopped fresh parsley

½ lemon

1. In a slow cooker, combine the olive oil, garlic, and onion. Cook on high, stirring occasionally, for 2 to 3 minutes, until fragrant. 2. Stir in the turkey, red bell pepper, yellow bell pepper, orange bell pepper, sweet potato, and zucchini. 3. Add the water, salt, black pepper, soy sauce, oregano, paprika, parsley, and a squeeze of lemon juice. Mix well. Cover, reduce the heat to low, and cook for 7 to 8 hours, until the turkey has cooked through and the vegetables are soft. 4. Serve the turkey and vegetables warm.

Per Serving: Calories 255; Fat 10g; Sodium 475mg; Carbs 2g; Fiber 1g; Sugar 0g; Protein 34g

Lemon & Garlicky Chicken Thighs

Prep time: 15 minutes | Cook time: 7-8 hours | Serves: 4-6

2 cups chicken broth

1½ teaspoons garlic powder

1 teaspoon sea salt

Juice and zest of 1 lemon

2 pounds boneless skinless chicken thighs

1. Pour the broth into the slow cooker. 2. In a bowl, stir the garlic powder, salt, lemon juice, and lemon zest. Baste each chicken thigh with an even coating of the mixture. Place the thighs along the bottom of the slow cooker. 3. Cover the slow cooker and set to low temp setting. Cook for 7 to 8 hours until the chicken juices run clear, and serve.

Per Serving: Calories 316; Fat 22g; Sodium 720mg; Carbs 0g; Fiber 0g; Sugar 0g; Protein 29g

Delicious Miso Chicken

Prep time: 20 minutes | Cook time: 7-8 hours | Serves: 8

1 onion, chopped

3 garlic cloves, minced

2 tablespoons grated fresh ginger root

2 pounds skinless chicken drumsticks

2 pounds skinless chicken thighs

2 cups Chicken stock, divided

2 tablespoons honey

2 tablespoons miso paste

2 tablespoons toasted sesame seeds

4 scallions, cut on the bias

1. In a slow cooker, mix the onion, garlic, and ginger root. Top with the chicken drumsticks and thighs. 2. In a bowl, mix ½ cup of the chicken stock with the honey and miso paste and whisk to blend. Add the remaining 1½ cups of the chicken stock and mix until well blended, then pour this mixture into the slow cooker. 3. Cover the slow cooker and cook on low temp setting for 7 to 8 hours. 4. Sprinkle with the sesame seeds and scallions and serve.

Per Serving: Calories 237; Fat 15g; Sodium 469mg; Carbs 2g; Fiber 1g; Sugar 1g; Protein 22g

Garlicky Parmesan Chicken

Prep time: 15 minutes | Cook time: 6 hours | Serves: 6

2 lb. chicken thighs, bone in

1 cup Parmesan cheese, grated

⅓ cup olive oil

5 garlic cloves, chopped

Seasoning: salt, pepper, thyme to taste

1. In a skillet, heat ⅓ cup olive oil and brown chicken on both sides, for 2-3 min each side. 2. Add chicken to a crockpot and spice with salt, pepper, garlic and thyme. 3. Close the lid and cook for 6 hours on low temp setting. 4. Open the lid, sprinkle with Parmesan and let sit for 15 minutes.

Per Serving: Calories 140; Fat 6g; Sodium 184mg; Carbs 0g; Fiber 0g; Sugar 0g; Protein 20g

Spicy BBQ Chicken

Prep time: 20 minutes | Cook time: 5-7 hours | Serves: 8

2 (8-ounce) BPA-free cans no-salt-added tomato sauce

2 onions, minced

8 garlic cloves, minced

⅓ cup mustard

2 tablespoons lemon juice

3 tablespoons molasses

1 tablespoon chili powder

2 teaspoons paprika

¼ teaspoon cayenne pepper

8 (6-ounce) boneless, skinless chicken breasts

1. In a slow cooker, mix the tomato sauce, onions, garlic, mustard, lemon juice, molasses, chili powder, paprika, and cayenne. 2. Add the chicken and use tongs to move the chicken around in the sauce to coat. Cover the slow cooker and cook on low temp setting for 5 to 7 hours.

Per Serving: Calories 156; Fat 7g; Sodium 404mg; Carbs 1g; Fiber 47.7g; Sugar 0g; Protein 21g

Delicious Turkey Sloppy Joes

Prep time: 15 minutes | Cook time: 4-6 hours | Serves: 4-6

1 tablespoon extra-virgin olive oil

1-pound ground turkey

1 celery stalk, minced

1 carrot, minced

½ medium sweet onion, diced

½ red bell pepper, finely chopped

6 tablespoons tomato paste

2 tablespoons apple cider vinegar

1 tablespoon maple syrup

1 teaspoon Dijon mustard

1 teaspoon chili powder

½ teaspoon garlic powder

½ teaspoon sea salt

½ teaspoon dried oregano

1. In slow cooker, combine the olive oil, turkey, celery, carrot, onion, red bell pepper, tomato paste, vinegar, maple syrup, mustard, chili powder, garlic powder, salt, and oregano. Using a spoon, break up the turkey into smaller chunks as it combines with the other ingredients. 2. Cover the slow cooker and set to low temp setting. Cook for 4 to 6 hours, stir thoroughly, and serve.

Per Serving: Calories 318; Fat 19g; Sodium 546mg; Carbs 4g; Fiber 0g; Sugar 2g; Protein 28g

Five-Spice Wings

Prep time: 15 minutes | Cook time: 6 hours | Serves: 4

16 chicken wings

2 tablespoons avocado oil

2 tablespoons Chinese five-spice

powder

1 jalapeño, sliced

Salt, pepper to taste

1. In a bowl, mix the wings with the oil, five-spice powder, salt and pepper. 2. Put the chicken wings into the slow cooker. Cook for 6 hours on low temp setting. Top with jalapeño and serve over rice.

Per Serving: Calories 416; Fat 26g; Sodium 666mg; Carbs 0g; Fiber 0g; Sugar 0g; Protein 36g

Turkey Meatballs

Prep time: 15 minutes | Cook time: 6-7 hours | Serves: 8

1 tablespoon extra-virgin olive oil

1-pound lean ground turkey

1 pound sweet Italian turkey sausage

¾ cup rolled oats

¼ cup grated Parmesan cheese, plus more for topping

3 eggs

¼ cup finely chopped fresh parsley, plus more for topping

¼ cup dried basil

½ teaspoon sea salt

½ teaspoon ground black pepper

2 teaspoons minced garlic

1 (28-ounce) jar no-sugar-added marinara sauce

1 (15-ounce) can crushed tomatoes

1 (15-ounce) can tomato sauce

1½ to 2 cups cooked whole-wheat pasta

1. Grease the bottom of a slow cooker with the olive oil. 2. In a bowl, combine the ground turkey, turkey sausage, oats, cheese, eggs, parsley, basil, salt, black pepper, and garlic. Stir. 3. Form the turkey mixture into 1½-inch balls. Arrange the balls in a single layer on the bottom of the slow cooker until the bottom is covered. 4. In a bowl, mix the marinara sauce, crushed tomatoes, and tomato sauce. 5. Pour one-third to half of the tomato mixture over top of the meatballs. 6. Repeat another layer of meatballs, and cover with the remaining sauce. Cover the slow cooker and cook on low temp setting for 6 to 7 hours, until the meatballs have cooked through. 7. Top with parsley and cheese. 8. Serve the meatballs warm over ¼ cup of pasta per serving.

Per Serving: Calories 432; Fat 22g; Sodium 623mg; Carbs 1g; Fiber 0g; Sugar 0g; Protein 48g

Prep time: 15 minutes | Cook time: 7-8 hours | Serves: 4-6

4 cups boneless, skinless turkey breast chunks

1 (14-ounce) can diced tomatoes

1 (14-ounce) can chickpeas, rinsed and drained well

2 carrots, finely chopped

½ cup dried apricots

½ red onion, chopped

2 tablespoons raw honey

1 tablespoon tomato paste

1 teaspoon garlic powder

1 teaspoon ground turmeric

½ teaspoon sea salt

¼ teaspoon ground ginger

¼ teaspoon ground coriander

¼ teaspoon paprika

½ cup water

2 cups broth of choice

Freshly ground black pepper

1. In slow cooker, combine the turkey, tomatoes, chickpeas, carrots, apricots, onion, honey, tomato paste, garlic powder, turmeric, salt, ginger, coriander, paprika, water, and broth, and Spice with pepper. Gently stir to blend the ingredients. 2. Cover the slow cooker and set to low temp setting. Cook for 7 to 8 hours and serve.

Per Serving: Calories 364; Fat 16g; Sodium 415mg; Carbs 3g; Fiber 1g; Sugar 1g; Protein 43g

Prep time: 15 minutes | Cook time: 6 hours | Serves: 8-10

1 tablespoon extra-virgin olive oil

3 to 3½ pounds boneless, skinless chicken thighs, cut into bite-size pieces

1 white onion, diced

1 tablespoon minced garlic

1½ tablespoons grated fresh ginger

1 tablespoon curry powder

1 tablespoon garam masala

2 teaspoons ground cumin

1 teaspoon cayenne pepper

1 teaspoon sea salt

½ teaspoon ground black pepper

1 teaspoon coconut sugar

2¼ cups coconut milk

1 (6-ounce) can tomato paste

2 to 2½ cups cooked wild or basmati rice

Plain Greek yogurt, for topping

Freshly squeezed lime juice, for topping

1. Grease the bottom of a slow cooker with the olive oil. 2. Add the chicken, onion, garlic, ginger, curry powder, garam masala, cumin, cayenne, salt, black pepper, sugar, coconut milk, and tomato paste. Mix well. 2. Cover the slow cooker and cook on low temp setting for 6 hours, until the chicken has cooked through. 3. Serve the chicken over ¼ cup of rice per serving. Top with a dollop of Greek yogurt and a squeeze of lime juice.

Per Serving: Calories 344; Fat 16g; Sodium 711mg; Carbs 0g; Fiber 0g; Sugar 0g; Protein 44g

Prep time: 15 minutes | Cook time: 8 hours | Serves: 8-10

1 tablespoon sea salt

1 teaspoon ground black pepper

2 teaspoons smoked paprika

½ teaspoon ground white pepper

½ teaspoon cayenne pepper

½ teaspoon garlic powder

½ teaspoon onion powder

½ teaspoon dried thyme

1 (5- to 6-pound) fresh whole chicken

1. To make the spice rub, in a bowl, combine the salt, black pepper, paprika, white pepper, cayenne, garlic powder, onion powder, and thyme. 2. Remove the giblets from inside the chicken, and use a paper towel to dry the interior. 3. Place 4 balls of aluminum foil in the bottom of a slow cooker. 4. Rub the outside and chicken with the spice rub, coating it well. 5. Place the chicken on the foil balls inside the slow cooker. Cover the slow cooker and cook on low temp setting for 8 hours, until the chicken is golden brown and cooked through. 6. Transfer the chicken to a rack or cutting board. Let rest for 5 minutes. 7. Slice the chicken and serve warm.

Per Serving: Calories 185; Fat 7g; Sodium 731mg; Carbs 1g; Fiber 0g; Sugar 0g; Protein 27g

White Bean and Chicken Chili

Prep time: 15 minutes | Cook time: 7-8 hours | Serves: 4-6

3 cups chopped cooked chicken

2 (15-ounce) cans white navy beans, rinsed well and drained

1 medium onion, chopped

1 (15-ounce) can diced tomatoes

3 cups Chicken Bone Broth or store-bought chicken broth

1 cup apple cider

2 bay leaves

1 tablespoon extra-virgin olive oil

2 teaspoons garlic powder

1 teaspoon chili powder

1 teaspoon sea salt

½ teaspoon ground cumin

¼ teaspoon ground cinnamon

Pinch cayenne pepper

Freshly ground black pepper

¼ cup apple cider vinegar

1. In slow cooker, combine the chicken, beans, onion, tomatoes, broth, cider, bay leaves, olive oil, garlic powder, chili powder, salt, cumin, cinnamon, and cayenne, and Spice with black pepper. 2. Cover the slow cooker and set to low temp setting. Cook for 7 to 8 hours. 3. Stir in the apple cider vinegar until well blended and serve.

Per Serving: Calories 164; Fat 8g; Sodium 397mg; Carbs 5g; Fiber 0g; Sugar 0g; Protein 16g

Prep time: 25 minutes | Cook time: 3 hours 20 minutes | Serves: 4

¼ cup butter

2 sweet onions, thinly sliced

1 teaspoon salt

½ teaspoon pepper

1 teaspoon chopped fresh thyme

4 boneless, skinless chicken breasts, cut

into small pieces

3 teaspoon cornstarch

2 teaspoons water

12 slices baguette, ½ inch thick (from 14-oz loaf)

½ cup shredded Swiss cheese (2 oz.)

1. In a skillet pan, melt butter over medium heat. Add onions, salt, pepper, and thyme, cook for 8 to 10 minutes, stirring properly, until onions are soft and golden brown. 2. Spoon onions into a 3½ to 4-quart slow cooker. Stir in chicken. Cover the slow cooker and cook on low temp setting for 2 to 3 hours or until chicken is no longer pink in center. 3. In a bowl, blend cornstarch with water. Stir into chicken mixture. Cover and cook on high temp setting 5 to 8 minutes or until thickened. 4. Meanwhile, set oven control to broil. Line a cookie sheet with foil. Arrange baguette slices in single layer on the cookie sheet. 5. Top baguette slices with cheese. Broil above the heat until cheese is melted and edges are golden brown. Serve with chicken.

Per Serving: Calories 388; Fat 14g; Sodium 1154mg; Carbs 3g; Fiber 0g; Sugar 0g; Protein 53g

Creamy Chicken and Sweet Peas

Prep time: 10 minutes | Cook time: 3 hours 30 minutes | Serves: 6

1 package (20 oz.) boneless, skinless chicken thighs (about 6)

¼ cup chicken broth

1 container (8 oz.) of chive and onion cream cheese spread

¼ teaspoon salt

½ teaspoon pepper

8 oz. chopped cooked bacon

1 cup frozen sweet peas

Cooked egg noodles, as desired

1. Spray the bottom of a 3-4 quart slow cooker with cooking spray. Add chicken thighs.
2. In a small microwavable bowl, mix chicken broth, cream cheese spread, salt and pepper, uncovered, microwave for 1 minute, and then beat with a whisk until smooth.
3. Pour this mixture on top of the chicken thighs. Cover the slow cooker and cook on low temp setting for 3 to 3½ hours. 4. Check for doneness, piercing the thickest part of the chicken. The juice of the chicken must be running clear. Stir ¾ cup of the bacon and the frozen sweet peas into the chicken mixture and mix well. 5. Increase the heat to high and cook 10 to 15 minutes longer or until the peas are cooked. Serve over the cooked egg noodles top with remaining ¼ cup bacon.

Per Serving: Calories 222; Fat 12g; Sodium 472mg; Carbs 1g; Fiber 0g; Sugar 0g; Protein 25g

Prep time: 15 minutes | Cook time: 4-6 hours | Serves: 4-6

1 tablespoon extra-virgin olive oil

1-pound ground turkey

3 cups sweet potato cubes

1 (28-ounce) can diced tomatoes

1 red bell pepper, diced

1 (4-ounce) can Hatch green chiles

½ medium red onion, diced

2 cups broth of choice

1 tablespoon freshly squeezed lime

juice

1 tablespoon chili powder

1 teaspoon garlic powder

1 teaspoon cocoa powder

1 teaspoon ground cumin

1 teaspoon sea salt

½ teaspoon ground cinnamon

Pinch cayenne pepper

1. In slow cooker, combine the olive oil, turkey, sweet potato cubes, tomatoes, bell pepper, chiles, onion, broth, lime juice, chili powder, garlic powder, cocoa powder, cumin, salt, cinnamon, and cayenne. 2. Break up the turkey into smaller chunks as it combines with the other ingredients. 3. Cover the slow cooker and set to low temp setting. Cook for 4 to 6 hours. 4. Stir the chili well, continuing to break up the rest of the turkey, and serve.

Per Serving: Calories 319; Fat 22g; Sodium 430mg; Carbs 1g; Fiber 0g; Sugar 0g; Protein 29g

Prep time: 20 minutes | Cook time: 4-6 hours | Serves: 8

2 leeks, chopped

3 garlic cloves, minced

2 (14-ounce) cans no-salt-added artichoke hearts, drained

2 red bell peppers, stemmed, seeded, and chopped

8 (6-ounce) boneless, skinless chicken breasts

1 cup Chicken Stock

2 tablespoons lemon juice

1 teaspoon dried basil leaves

½ cup chopped flat-leaf parsley

1. In a slow cooker, layer the leeks, garlic, artichoke hearts, bell peppers, chicken, stock, lemon juice, and basil. 2. Cover the slow cooker and cook on low temp setting for 4 to 6 hours until the chicken is tender. 3. Sprinkle with the parsley and serve.

Per Serving: Calories 533; Fat 30g; Sodium 845mg; Carbs 3g; Fiber 0g; Sugar 0g; Protein 52g

Beef and Barley Stew

Prep time: 15 minutes | Cook time: 8 hours | Serves: 8-10

2 pounds stew beef, cut into bite-size cubes

½ teaspoon sea salt, plus more for seasoning

½ teaspoon ground black pepper, plus more for Seasoning

3 tablespoons extra-virgin olive oil

1 cup sliced carrots

1 onion, diced

2 white potatoes (skin on), cut into bite-size pieces

4 teaspoons minced garlic

6 cups beef broth

1½ cups pearled barley

2 teaspoons dried thyme

½ teaspoon dried rosemary

¼ cup tomato paste

1 tablespoon Worcestershire sauce

1 or 2 bay leaves

1 to 1¼ cups plain 2 percent Greek yogurt, for topping

Chopped fresh parsley, for topping

1. Season the beef with salt and black pepper. 2. Grease the bottom of a slow cooker with the olive oil. 3. Set the heat to high. Add the beef and cook, stirring occasionally, for 3 to 4 minutes. 4. Add the carrots, onion, potatoes, garlic, broth, barley, thyme, rosemary, tomato paste, Worcestershire sauce, salt, black pepper, and bay leaf. Mix well. Cover, reduce the heat to low, and cook for 8 hours. 5. Top with 2 tablespoons of Greek yogurt per serving and parsley. Serve the stew warm.

Per Serving: Calories 393; Fat 23g; Sodium 1148mg; Carbs 7.5g; Fiber 2.4g; Sugar 1.4g; Protein 29.5g

Spicy Pork Ragù

Prep time: 15 minutes | Cook time: 7-8 hours | Serves: 4-6

1-pound pork tenderloin

1 medium yellow onion, diced

1 red bell pepper, diced

1 (28-ounce) can diced tomatoes

2 teaspoons chili powder

1 teaspoon garlic powder

½ teaspoon ground cumin

½ teaspoon smoked paprika

Dash red pepper flakes

1 cup fresh spinach leaves, minced

1. In slow cooker, combine the pork, onion, bell pepper, tomatoes, chili powder, garlic powder, cumin, paprika, red pepper flakes, and spinach. 2. Cover the slow cooker and set to low temp setting. Cook for 7 to 8 hours. 3. Transfer the pork loin to a cutting board and shred with a fork. Return it to the slow cooker, stir it into the sauce, and serve.

Per Serving: Calories 574; Fat 40.4g; Sodium 557mg; Carbs 9.6g; Fiber 1.7g; Sugar 6.3g; Protein 32.7g

Herbed Balsamic Lamb Chops

Prep time: 15 minutes | Cook time: 7-8 hours | Serves: 4-6

1 medium onion, sliced

2 teaspoons garlic powder

2 teaspoons dried rosemary

1 teaspoon sea salt

½ teaspoon dried thyme leaves

Freshly ground black pepper

8 bone-in lamb chops (about 3 pounds)

2 tablespoons balsamic vinegar

1. Line the bottom of the slow cooker with the onion slices. 2. In a bowl, stir the garlic powder, rosemary, salt, thyme, and pepper. Rub the chops evenly with the spice mixture, and gently place them in the slow cooker. 3. Drizzle the vinegar over the top. 4. Cover the slow cooker and set to low temp setting. Cook for 7 to 8 hours and serve.

Per Serving: Calories 476; Fat 33.5g; Sodium 860mg; Carbs 4.3g; Fiber 1.3g; Sugar 1.3g; Protein 29.9g

Lemon–Garlicky Pork Chops

Prep time: 20 minutes | Cook time: 7-8 hours | Serves: 8

2 leeks, chopped

8 garlic cloves, sliced

2 red bell peppers, stemmed, seeded, and chopped

8 (5-ounce) bone-in pork loin chops

⅓ cup lemon juice

1 cup Chicken Stock

1 teaspoon dried thyme leaves

½ teaspoon salt

1. In a slow cooker, mix the leeks, garlic, and red bell peppers. Top with the pork chops. 2. In a bowl, mix the lemon juice, chicken stock, thyme, and salt. Pour over the pork. 3. Cover the slow cooker and cook on low temp setting for 7 to 8 hours.

Per Serving: Calories 544; Fat 44g; Sodium 933mg; Carbs 0g; Fiber 0g; Sugar 0g; Protein 35g

Spicy Chili–Lime Pork Tenderloins

Prep time: 15 minutes | Cook time: 6-7 hours | Serves: 4-6

3 teaspoons chili powder

2 teaspoons garlic powder

1 teaspoon ground cumin

½ teaspoon sea salt

2 (1-pound) pork tenderloins

1 cup broth of choice

¼ cup freshly squeezed lime juice

1. In a bowl, stir the chili powder, garlic powder, cumin, and salt. Rub the pork all over with the spice mixture, and put it in the slow cooker. 2. Pour the broth and lime juice around the pork in the cooker. 3. Cover the slow cooker and set to low temp setting. Cook for 6 to 7 hours. 4. Remove the pork from the slow cooker and let rest for 5 minutes. Slice the pork against the grain into medallions before serving.

Per Serving: Calories 340; Fat 20.3g; Sodium 851mg; Carbs 5.6g; Fiber 1.5g; Sugar 1.8g; Protein 26.4g

Curried Pork Chops

Prep time: 20 minutes | Cook time: 7-8 hours | Serves: 8

2 onions, chopped

4 garlic cloves, minced

2 red bell peppers, stemmed, seeded, and chopped

2 yellow bell peppers, stemmed, seeded, and chopped

8 (5.5-ounce) bone-in pork loin chops

½ teaspoon salt

1 tablespoon curry powder

1 tablespoon grated fresh ginger root

1 cup Chicken Stock

1. In a slow cooker, mix the onions, garlic, and bell peppers. Add the pork chops to the slow cooker, nestling them into the vegetables. 2 In a bowl, mix the salt, curry powder, ginger root, and chicken stock, and pour into the slow cooker. 3. Cover the slow cooker and cook on low temp setting for 7 to 8 hours until the pork chops are very tender.

Per Serving: Calories 429; Fat 27.3g; Sodium 836mg; Carbs 6.6g; Fiber 3.4g; Sugar 1.9g; Protein 29.2g

Roast Pork and Cabbage

Prep time: 20 minutes | Cook time: 7-9 hours | Serves: 8

1 head red cabbage, chopped

2 red onions, chopped

2 medium pears, peeled and chopped

4 garlic cloves, minced

1 cup Chicken Stock

¼ cup apple cider vinegar

3 tablespoons honey

1 teaspoon dried thyme leaves

½ teaspoon salt

1 (3-pound) pork loin roast

1. In a slow cooker, mix the cabbage, onions, pears, and garlic. 2. In a bowl, mix the chicken stock, vinegar, honey, thyme, and salt, and pour into the slow cooker. 3. Top with the pork, nestling the meat into the vegetables. 4. Cover the slow cooker and cook on low temp setting for 7 to 9 hours until the pork is tender.

Per Serving: Calories 338; Fat 18g; Sodium 788mg; Carbs 14g; Fiber 5g; Sugar 2g; Protein 28g

Beef & Mushroom Noodles

Prep time: 25 minutes | Cook time: 25 minutes | Serves: 10

1 lb. lean (at least 80%) ground beef

2 packages (8 oz. each) of sliced button mushrooms

1 can (12 oz.) evaporated milk

1 lb. uncooked medium egg noodles

1 container (12 oz.) of chive and onion sour cream

4½ cups hot water

Salt, to taste

1. In a slow cooker, brown beef over high heat. Stir frequently. Add mushrooms and salt to taste. Cook about 5 minutes. 2. Add 1 can milk, 4½ cups hot water and the noodles. Heat to boiling over high heat. 3. Lower the heat and simmer uncovered for 7 to 8 minutes, stirring frequently. Remove from heat when the noodles are tender.

Per Serving: Calories 481; Fat 38g; Sodium 941mg; Carbs 5g; Fiber 3g; Sugar 2g; Protein 29g

Beef Roast with Mushroom & Carrot

Prep time: 20 minutes | Cook time: 8-10 hours | Serves: 8

2 onions, sliced

4 garlic cloves, sliced

2 shallots, peeled and sliced

2 cups sliced cremini mushrooms

5 carrots, sliced

1 (3-pound) grass-fed chuck shoulder

roast or tri-tip roast, cut into 2-inch pieces

2 tablespoons chopped fresh chives

1 teaspoon dried marjoram leaves

1 cup low-sodium beef broth

2 tablespoons butter

1. In a slow cooker, mix the onions, garlic, shallots, mushrooms, and carrots. 2. Add the beef and stir gently. Sprinkle the chives and marjoram over the beef, and pour the beef broth over all. 3. Cover the slow cooker and cook on low temp setting for 8 to 10 hours until the beef is very tender. 4. Stir in the butter and serve.

Per Serving: Calories 263; Fat 14.6g; Sodium 671mg; Carbs 7.7g; Fiber 1.2g; Sugar 2.4g; Protein 22.2g

Thai-style Pork with Peanut Sauce

Prep time: 20 minutes | Cook time: 7-9 hours | Serves: 8

2 onions, chopped

2 cups chopped portobello mushrooms

4 garlic cloves, minced

1 small dried red chili pepper, sliced

¼ teaspoon cayenne pepper

1 cup peanut butter

1 cup Chicken Stock

2 tablespoons apple cider vinegar

1 (3-pound) boneless pork loin roast

1 cup chopped unsalted peanuts

1. In a slow cooker, mix the onions, mushrooms, garlic, chili pepper, and cayenne pepper. 2. In a bowl, mix the peanut butter, chicken stock, and vinegar and mix until well blended. 3. Place the pork roast in the slow cooker on top of the vegetables. Pour the peanut butter sauce over all. 4. Cover the slow cooker and cook on low temp setting for 7 to 9 hours until the pork is very tender. 5. Sprinkle with peanuts and serve.

Per Serving: Calories 531; Fat 29g; Sodium 1036mg; Carbs 6g; Fiber 2g; Sugar 2g; Protein 50g

Beef Roast and Sweet Potatoes

Prep time: 15 minutes | Cook time: 7-8 hours | Serves: 6-8

1 teaspoon sea salt

1½ teaspoons dried thyme leaves

1 teaspoon dried rosemary

½ teaspoon freshly ground black pepper

1 (4-pound) beef chuck roast

1 medium onion, sliced

5 carrots, chopped

1 celery stalk, chopped

6 garlic cloves, minced

2 cups broth of choice

3 bay leaves

2 sweet potatoes, peeled and cubed

1. In a bowl, stir the salt, thyme, rosemary, and pepper. Rub the spices all over the roast. Set aside. 2. In slow cooker, layer the onion, carrots, celery, and garlic on the bottom. 3. Add the broth and bay leaves. Put the meat on top of the vegetables. 4. Put the sweet potatoes on top of the meat. 5. Cover the slow cooker and set to low temp setting. Cook for 7 to 8 hours. 6. Remove and discard the bay leaves before serving.

Per Serving: Calories 421; Fat 23.4g; Sodium 990mg; Carbs 4.8g; Fiber 1.3g; Sugar 1.2g; Protein 39.5g

Prep time: 15 minutes | Cook time: 7½-8 hours | Serves: 8

2 tablespoons extra-virgin olive oil

2 pounds' stew beef, cut into 1-inch cubes

Sea salt

Ground black pepper

1-pound fingerling potatoes, peeled and halved (3½ cups)

2 cups baby carrots

1 small onion, diced

3 tablespoons minced garlic

3 cups beef broth

1 (6-ounce) can tomato paste

1 teaspoon dried thyme

⅓ cup potato flakes

Chopped fresh parsley, for garnish

1. Grease the bottom of a slow cooker with the olive oil. 2. Set the heat to high. Add the beef. Season with salt and black pepper. Sauté for 3 to 4 minutes, until browned. 3. Add the potatoes, carrots, onion, and garlic. Mix well. Stir in the broth, tomato paste, and thyme. Season with salt and black pepper. Mix well. 4. Cover, reduce the heat to low, and cook for 7 hours, until the vegetables are soft. 5. Remove the lid and stir in the potato flakes. Replace the lid and cook for 30 minutes to 1 hour, until thickened. 6. Serve the stew warm, garnished with parsley. 7. Refrigerate leftovers for up to 1 week, or freeze for up to 2 months.

Per Serving: Calories139; Fat 5.8g; Sodium 467mg; Carbs 7.1g; Fiber 2.6g; Sugar 3.5g; Protein 12.8g

Prep time: 15 minutes | Cook time: 6 hours | Serves: 6-8

1 tablespoon extra-virgin olive oil

1 pound 85% lean ground beef

1-pound ground pork

1 (28-ounce) can tomato sauce

1 (28-ounce) can crushed tomatoes

1 (6-ounce) can tomato paste

1 medium yellow onion, diced

1 yellow or orange bell pepper, cored and diced

3 tablespoons minced garlic

1 cup beef broth

2 tablespoons chili powder

1 teaspoon cayenne pepper

½ teaspoon sea salt

½ teaspoon ground black pepper

Chopped fresh cilantro, sliced scallions, or sliced avocado, for topping

¾ to 1 cup sour cream, for topping

¾ to 1 cup guacamole, for topping

1. Grease the bottom of a slow cooker with the olive oil. 2. Set the heat to high. Add the beef and pork. Cook, stirring occasionally, for 2 to 3 minutes. 3. Add the tomato sauce, crushed tomatoes, tomato paste, onion, bell pepper, garlic, broth, chili powder, cayenne, salt, and black pepper. Stir. Cover, reduce the heat to low, and cook for 6 hours, until the pork has cooked through and the vegetables are soft. 4. Top with cilantro, scallions, or avocado, 2 tablespoons of sour cream per serving or 2 tablespoons of guacamole per serving. Do not add scallions if you are at the soft-foods stage. Serve the chili warm.

Per Serving: Calories 272; Fat 19.1g; Sodium 516mg; Carbs 1.3g; Fiber 0.7g; Sugar 0.1g; Protein 18.3g

Prep time: 15 minutes | Cook time: 7-8 hours | Serves: 6-8

2 tablespoons extra-virgin olive oil

3 to 4 pounds' lamb shoulder, trimmed of excess fat

1 cup beef broth or chicken broth

1 cup aged balsamic vinegar

1 tablespoon onion powder

⅔ cup pure maple syrup

1 teaspoon minced garlic

1 tablespoon dried oregano

2 teaspoons dried sage

1 teaspoon sea salt

1 teaspoon ground black pepper

2 tablespoons feta cheese, for topping

Arugula, for topping

1. Grease the bottom of a slow cooker with the olive oil. Heat on low for 2 to 3 minutes. 2. Place the lamb in the slow cooker, with the fattiest part on top. 3. Add the broth, vinegar, onion powder, maple syrup, garlic, oregano, sage, salt, and black pepper on top of the lamb, letting the liquid fall over the sides of the lamb. 4. Cover the slow cooker and cook on low temp setting for 7 to 8 hours, until the lamb is tender and cooked through. 5. Remove the lid and transfer the lamb to a cutting board or platter. Cut it into 1- to 2-inch chunks, or shred it using 2 forks. 6. Return it to the slow cooker and stir. Replace the lid and cook for 5 to 10 minutes. 7. Top with the cheese and arugula. Serve the lamb warm.

Per Serving: Calories 442; Fat 29.8g; Sodium 575mg; Carbs 2.4g; Fiber 0.4g; Sugar 1.1g; Protein 29.8g

Tangy Honey Mustard Pork Roast

Prep time: 10 minutes | Cook time: 7-8 hours | Serves: 8

1 onion, chopped

4 cloves garlic, minced

⅓ cup honey mustard

1 teaspoon salt

¼ teaspoon pepper

1 teaspoon dried thyme

3-lb pork roast

¼ cup chicken broth

1 tablespoon cornstarch

¼ cup water

1. Grease a slow cooker with cooking spray and add onions and garlic. Rub salt and pepper and honey mustard over the pork roast. Sprinkle with thyme. Place coated roast on top of onions and garlic. 2. Pour the chicken broth. Cover the slow cooker and cook on low for 7–8 hours. 3. Remove roast and cover with foil while making the sauce. 4. Combine the cornstarch and water in a medium saucepan and blend with a wire whisk. 5. Add juices from the slow cooker and the cooked onions and garlic to the saucepan. Cook over medium heat, stirring. 6. Remove the heat when the mixture thickens. Season to taste. Add more salt, pepper, thyme, or honey mustard if needed. A slow cooker mutes these flavors because of its long cooking time. Slice the roast and serve it with the sauce.

Per Serving: Calories 565; Fat 49g; Sodium 753mg; Carbs 0g; Fiber 0g; Sugar 0g; Protein 28g

Prep time: 15 minutes | Cook time: 7-8 hours | Serves: 4-6

1 teaspoon sea salt

1 teaspoon ground cumin

1 teaspoon garlic powder

½ teaspoon dried oregano

½ teaspoon freshly ground black pepper

3 to 4 pounds pork shoulder or butt

2 cups broth of choice

Juice of 1 orange

1 small onion, chopped

4 to 6 corn taco shells

Shredded cabbage, lime wedges, avocado, and hot sauce, for topping

1. In a bowl, stir the salt, cumin, garlic powder, oregano, and pepper. Rub the pork with the spice mixture, and put it in slow cooker. 2. Pour the broth and orange juice around the pork. Scatter the onion around the pork. 3. Cover the slow cooker and set on low. Cook for 7 to 8 hours. 4. Transfer the pork to a work surface, and shred it with a fork. Serve in taco shells with any optional toppings you like.

Per Serving: Calories 628; Fat 37.9g; Sodium 1002mg; Carbs 28.6g; Fiber 5.6g; Sugar 12.1g; Protein 36.5g

Chicken and Rice Soup

Prep time: 15 minutes | Cook time: 7 hours | Serves: 6-8

1 cup wild rice, rinsed and drained

1½ pounds boneless, skinless chicken breasts

2 cups sliced carrots

1 cup sliced celery

1 small yellow onion, diced

4 teaspoons minced garlic

1 teaspoon dried rosemary

1 teaspoon dried thyme

2 teaspoons sea salt

½ teaspoon ground black pepper

1 or 2 bay leaves

6 cups Savory Chicken Broth or store-bought chicken broth

3 tablespoons extra-virgin olive oil

2 cups unsweetened almond or oat milk

½ cup whole-wheat flour

Chopped fresh parsley, fresh thyme, or freshly squeezed lemon or lime juice, for topping

1. In a slow cooker, combine the rice, chicken, carrots, celery, onion, garlic, rosemary, thyme, salt, black pepper, bay leaf, and broth. Cover the slow cooker and cook on low temp setting for 7 hours, until the chicken has cooked through and the vegetables are soft. 2. Remove the lid and remove the chicken. Shred the chicken by using 2 forks. Return the meat to the slow cooker and stir. 3. In a bowl, whisk the olive oil, milk, and flour until any lumps have dissolved and the mixture is thick and creamy. Pour into the slow cooker and mix well. 4. Serve the soup warm, garnished with parsley, thyme, or lemon juice.

Per Serving: Calories 247; Fat 26g; Sodium 145mg; Carbs 0g; Fiber 0g; Sugar 0g; Protein 0g

Lentil–Barley and Kale Soup

Prep time: 20 minutes | Cook time: 6-7 hours | Serves: 8

2 onions, chopped

1 leek, chopped

4 garlic cloves, minced

4 carrots, peeled and sliced

3 tomatoes, seeded and chopped

1½ cups pearl barley

1½ cups pay lentils

12 cups Roasted Vegetable Broth

1 teaspoon dried dill weed

2 cups chopped kale

1. In a slow cooker, mix the onions, leek, garlic, carrots, tomatoes, barley, lentils, vegetable broth, and dill weed. Cover the slow cooker and cook on low temp setting for 6 to 7 hours until the barley and lentils are tender. 2. Stir in the kale; cover the slow cooker and cook on low temp setting for 15 to 20 minutes until the kale has wilted.

Per Serving: Calories 275; Fat 24g; Sodium 255mg; Carbs 4g; Fiber 31g; Sugar 2g; Protein 8g

Spicy Bean and Corn Soup

Prep time: 20 minutes | Cook time: 8-9 hours | Serves: 8

3 cups dried black beans

2 onions, chopped

4 tomatoes, seeded and chopped

6 garlic cloves, minced

2 jalapeño peppers, minced

3 cups frozen corn

2 tablespoons chili powder

1 teaspoon ground red chili

1 teaspoon ground cumin

11 cups Roasted Vegetable Broth

1. In a slow cooker, mix all of the ingredients. 2. Cover the slow cooker and cook on low temp setting for 8 to 9 hours until the beans are tender.

Per Serving: Calories 169; Fat 11g; Sodium 713mg; Carbs 7g; Fiber 2g; Sugar 4g; Protein 11g

Beans and French Onion Soup

Prep time: 15 minutes | Cook time: 3-4 hours | Serves: 4-6

2 onions, thinly sliced

¼ cup extra-virgin olive oil

¾ teaspoon sea salt

2 (14-ounce) cans cannellini beans, rinsed and drained well

4 cups vegetable broth

½ teaspoon garlic powder

½ teaspoon dried thyme leaves

1 bay leaf

Freshly ground black pepper

1. In slow cooker, combine the onions, olive oil, and salt. 2. Cover the slow cooker and set to high. Cook for 3 hours, allowing the onions to caramelize. 3. Stir the onions well and add the beans, broth, garlic powder, thyme, and bay leaf, and Spice with pepper. 4. Re-cover the cooker and set to low temp setting. Cook for 4 hours. 5. Remove before serving.

Per Serving: Calories 237; Fat 15g; Sodium 818mg; Carbs 13g; Fiber 5g; Sugar 3g; Protein 17g

Vegetable and Wild Rice Chili

Prep time: 20 minutes | Cook time: 6-7 hours | Serves: 8

1½ cups wild rice, rinsed and drained

2 onions, chopped

3 garlic cloves, minced

2 cups sliced cremini mushrooms

2 red bell peppers, stemmed, seeded, and chopped

2 (15-ounce) BPA-free cans no-salt-added black beans, drained and rinsed

1 tablespoon chili powder

½ teaspoon ground cumin

5 cups Roasted Vegetable Broth

3 cups low-sodium tomato juice

1. In a slow cooker, mix all of the ingredients. 2. Cover the slow cooker and cook on low temp setting for 6 to 7 hours until the wild rice is tender.

Per Serving: Calories 204; Fat 14g; Sodium 111mg; Carbs 13g; Fiber 7g; Sugar 3g; Protein 10g

Easy Roasted Vegetable Broth

Prep time: 20 minutes | Cook time: 6-8 hours | Serves: 12

2 onions, peeled and chopped
1 leek, chopped
3 carrots, cut into 2-inch pieces
2 celery stalks, cut into 2-inch pieces
4 garlic cloves, smashed
1 tablespoon olive oil

1 tablespoon freshly squeezed lemon juice
1 bay leaf
½ teaspoon salt
10 cups water

1. In a roasting pan, mix the onions, leek, carrots, celery, and garlic. Drizzle with the olive oil and toss to coat. Roast at 375°F for 15 to 20 minutes until the vegetables are light brown. 2. In a slow cooker, add the vegetables and remaining ingredients. Cover the slow cooker and cook on low for 6 to 8 hours. 3. Remove the solids using tongs and discard. Strain the broth through cheesecloth into a bowl.

Per Serving: Calories 217; Fat 18g; Sodium 948mg; Carbs 8g; Fiber 2g; Sugar 3g; Protein 4g

Warm Beef Stock

Prep time: 15 minutes | Cook time: 9-12 hours | Serves: 4-6

4 pounds beef bones
3 carrots, cut into 2-inch chunks
2 celery stalks, cut into 2-inch pieces
2 onions, cut into 8 wedges each
3 garlic cloves, peeled and smashed
1 tablespoon freshly squeezed lemon

juice
1 teaspoon black peppercorns
1 teaspoon salt
1 bay leaf
12 cups water

1. For the richest flavor, brown the beef bones before you make the stock. In a roasting pan, bake at 375°F for 30 to 40 minutes until they are browned. 2. In a slow cooker, add the bones and remaining ingredients. Cover the slow cooker and cook on low for 9 to 12 hours until the stock is a rich brown color. 3. Remove the solids using tongs and discard. Strain the stock through cheesecloth into a bowl.

Per Serving: Calories 362; Fat 23g; Sodium 403mg; Carbs 15g; Fiber 8g; Sugar 3g; Protein 23g

Carrot–Barley Soup

Prep time: 20 minutes | Cook time: 8 hours | Serves: 8

1½ cups hulled barley

1 bunch (about 6) carrots, cut into 2-inch chunks and tops reserved

1 celery root, peeled and cubed

2 onions, chopped

5 garlic cloves, minced

8 cups Roasted Vegetable Broth (here)

2 cups bottled unsweetened carrot juice

1 teaspoon dried dill weed

1 bay leaf

2 tablespoons freshly squeezed lemon juice

1. In a slow cooker, mix the barley, carrots, celery root, onions, and garlic. 2. Add the vegetable broth, carrot juice, dill weed, and bay leaf. 3. Cover the slow cooker and cook on low temp setting for 8 to 9 hours until the barley and vegetables are tender. Remove. 4. Chop the carrot tops and add 1 cup to the slow cooker. Add the lemon juice. Cover the slow cooker and cook on low temp setting for another 15 minutes.

Per Serving: Calories 347; Fat 23g; Sodium 699mg; Carbs 8g; Fiber 2g; Sugar 5g; Protein 25g

Tangy Vegetable Broth

Prep time: 10 minutes | Cook time: 8-10 hours | Serves: 6

8 carrots, sliced

2 cups chopped celery

2 medium yellow onions, diced

2 cups sliced cremini mushrooms

2 teaspoons sea salt

1 teaspoon ground black pepper

6 cups water

1. In a slow cooker, combine the carrots, celery, onions, mushrooms, salt, black pepper, and water. Cover the slow cooker and cook on low temp setting for 8 to 10 hours, until heated through. 2. Strain the vegetables over a container and discard them. 3. Serve the broth warm, or use it in other recipes.

Per Serving: Calories 106; Fat 4g; Sodium 1035mg; Carbs 12g; Fiber 4g; Sugar 4g; Protein 7g

Prep time: 10 minutes | Cook time: 6 hours | Serves: 4

2 tablespoons coconut oil

2 cups cauliflower florets

8 ounces' firm tofu, cut into 1-inch cubes

½ onion, diced

2 cups crumbled blue cheese, divided

1 cup diced tomatoes, with juice

¼ cup all-natural spicy hot sauce

1 tablespoon erythritol

1½ teaspoons chili powder

1 teaspoon ground cumin

¼ teaspoon kosher salt

2 celery stalks, finely diced

1. In the slow cooker, combine the coconut oil, cauliflower, tofu, onion, 1 cup of blue cheese, tomatoes and their juice, hot sauce, erythritol, chili powder, cumin, and salt. Stir to mix. Cover and cook for 6 hours on low temp setting. 2. Serve the chili hot, topped with the celery and remaining 1 cup of blue cheese.

Per Serving: Calories 354; Fat 7.9g; Sodium 704mg; Carbs 6g; Fiber 3.6g; Sugar 6g; Protein 18g

Prep time: 15 minutes | Cook time: 7½ -8 hours | Serves: 10

3 pounds fingerling potatoes, peeled and halved

2 teaspoons minced garlic

1 small white onion, chopped

1½ teaspoons sea salt

½ teaspoon ground black pepper

4 cups Savory Chicken Broth

2 cups 2 percent milk

1 cup shredded Cheddar cheese

1. In a slow cooker, combine the potatoes, garlic, onion, salt, black pepper, and broth. 2. Cover the slow cooker and cook on low temp setting for 7 hours, until the potatoes are soft. 3. Remove the lid and stir in the milk and cheese. Replace the lid and cook for 30 minutes to 1 hour, until the soup is heated through and the cheese has melted. 4. Using a blender, blend the soup until smooth. Pour through a strainer into a container, and discard any lumps or bits. Serve warm.

Per Serving: Calories 627; Fat 44g; Sodium 1491mg; Carbs 5g; Fiber 1g; Sugar 3g; Protein 41g

Sweet Potato & Almond Soup

Prep time: 15 minutes | Cook time: 6-8 hours | Serves: 4-6

4 cups vegetable broth, plus more if needed

1 (15-ounce) can diced tomatoes

2 medium sweet potatoes, peeled and diced

1 medium onion, diced

1 jalapeño pepper, seeded and diced

½ cup unsalted almond butter

½ teaspoon sea salt

½ teaspoon garlic powder

½ teaspoon ground turmeric

½ teaspoon ground ginger

¼ teaspoon ground cinnamon

Pinch ground nutmeg

½ cup full-fat coconut milk

1. In slow cooker, combine the broth, tomatoes, sweet potatoes, onion, jalapeño, almond butter, salt, garlic powder, turmeric, ginger, cinnamon, and nutmeg. 2. Cover the slow cooker and set to low temp setting. Cook for 6 to 8 hours. 3. Stir in the coconut milk after cooking. 4. Using a blender, purée the soup until smooth and serve.

Per Serving: Calories 307; Fat 16g; Sodium 1089mg; Carbs 6g; Fiber 2g; Sugar 3g; Protein 26g

Savory Chicken and Carrot Broth

Prep time: 10 minutes | Cook time: 8-10 hours | Serves: 6

3 pounds bone-in chicken pieces

4 carrots, sliced

1 cup chopped celery

1 medium yellow onion, diced

2 teaspoons minced garlic

1 teaspoon dried thyme

1 teaspoon dried parsley

1 teaspoon dried oregano

1 teaspoon dried rosemary

2 teaspoons sea salt

1 teaspoon ground black pepper

6 cups water

1. In a slow cooker, combine the chicken, carrots, celery, onion, garlic, thyme, parsley, oregano, rosemary, salt, black pepper, and water. Cover the slow cooker and cook on low temp setting for 8 to 10 hours, until heated through. 2. Strain the solids over a heat-safe container and discard the vegetables. 3. If desired, pull the chicken meat off the bones and add back to the broth for more protein. 4. Serve the broth warm, or use it in other recipes.

Per Serving: Calories 306; Fat 28g; Sodium 283mg; Carbs 11g; Fiber 6g; Sugar 5g; Protein 5g

Thai–style Curry Vegetable Soup

Prep time: 15 minutes | Cook time: 6-8 hours | Serves: 4-6

4 cups vegetable broth
½ cup sliced mushrooms
3 carrots, diced
1 bunch baby bok choy
1 sweet potato, peeled and diced
1 small head broccoli, florets chopped
1 small onion, diced
1 lemongrass stalk, chopped into 1-inch segments

1 tablespoon freshly squeezed lime juice
1 tablespoon curry paste
2 teaspoons fish sauce
¾ teaspoon sea salt
½ teaspoon ground ginger
½ teaspoon garlic powder
¾ cup full-fat coconut milk
Fresh cilantro leaves, for garnishing

1. In slow cooker, stir the broth, mushrooms, carrots, bok choy, sweet potato, broccoli, onion, lemongrass, lime juice, curry paste, fish sauce, salt, ginger, and garlic powder. 2. Cover the slow cooker and set to low temp setting. Cook for 6 to 8 hours. 3. Stir in the coconut milk and garnish with the cilantro before serving.

Per Serving: Calories 240; Fat 10g; Sodium 350mg; Carbs 14g; Fiber 5g; Sugar 4g; Protein 24g

Healthy Beans and Vegetables Soup

Prep time: 15 minutes | Cook time: 6-8 hours | Serves: 4-6

1 (14-ounce) can diced tomatoes with their juice
1 (14-ounce) can kidney beans, drained and rinsed well
2 celery stalks, diced
2 carrots, diced
1 zucchini, diced
1 small onion, diced
1 tablespoon freshly squeezed lemon

juice
1 teaspoon sea salt
½ teaspoon garlic powder
½ teaspoon dried oregano
½ teaspoon dried basil leaves
½ teaspoon dried rosemary
2 bay leaves
6 cups vegetable broth
1 cup packed fresh spinach

1. In slow cooker, combine the tomatoes, kidney beans, celery, carrots, zucchini, onion, lemon juice, salt, garlic powder, oregano, basil, rosemary, bay leaves, and broth. 2. Cover the slow cooker and set to low temp setting. Cook for 6 to 8 hours. 3. Stir in the spinach and let wilt before serving.

Per Serving: Calories 153; Fat 5g; Sodium 348mg; Carbs 10g; Fiber 4g; Sugar 5g; Protein 16g

Prep time: 15 minutes | Cook time: 7 hours | Serves: 6-8

4½ cups savory chicken broth

1 cup sliced carrots

1 (8-ounce) can bamboo shoots, drained

1 (8-ounce) can water chestnuts, drained

1 (4-ounce) can sliced mushrooms, drained

¼ cup rice vinegar

4 teaspoons low-sodium soy sauce or

coconut aminos

1 teaspoon coconut sugar

½ teaspoon red pepper flakes

2 tablespoons arrowroot starch

2 tablespoons water

8 ounces' pork shoulder or loin, sliced

4 to 6 ounces firm tofu, drained and cubed

Sliced scallions, for topping

1. In a slow cooker, combine the broth, carrots, bamboo shoots, water chestnuts, mushrooms, vinegar, soy sauce, sugar, and red pepper flakes. Cover the slow cooker and cook on low temp setting for 7 hours. 2. In a bowl, mix the arrowroot starch and water to make a slurry. 3. Remove the slow cooker lid and add the slurry, pork, and tofu. Cover, increase the heat to high, and cook for 30 minutes. 4. Garnish with scallions, and serve the soup warm.

Per Serving: Calories 280; Fat 15g; Sodium 673mg; Carbs 8g; Fiber 3g; Sugar 4g; Protein 24g

Salted Drinking Chocolate

Prep time: 15 minutes | Cook time: 3-4 hours | Serves: 4-6

5 cups unsweetened almond milk

2½ tablespoons coconut oil

5 tablespoons cacao powder

5 cinnamon sticks

3 to 4 teaspoons coconut sugar or raw honey

1 tablespoon vanilla extract

1 (3-inch) piece fresh ginger

1 (2-inch) piece turmeric root

3 tablespoons collagen peptides

½ to ¾ teaspoon sea salt, divided

1. In slow cooker, combine the almond milk, coconut oil, cacao powder, cinnamon sticks, coconut sugar or honey, vanilla, ginger, and turmeric. 2. Cover the slow cooker and set to low temp setting. Cook for 3 to 4 hours. 3. Pour the contents of the cooker through a fine-mesh sieve into a clean container; discard the solids. 4. Stir in the collagen peptides until well combined. 5. Pour the chocolate into mugs and gently sprinkle ⅛ teaspoon of sea salt on top of each beverage. Serve hot.

Per Serving: Calories 217; Fat 18g; Sodium 71mg; Carbs 19g; Fiber 8g; Sugar 0g; Protein 8g

Aromatic Cinnamon Pecans

Prep time: 15 minutes | Cook time: 3-4 hours | Serves: 4

1 tablespoon coconut oil

1 egg white

2 tablespoons ground cinnamon

2 teaspoons vanilla extract

¼ cup maple syrup

2 tablespoons coconut sugar

¼ teaspoon sea salt

3 cups pecan halves

1. Grease the slow cooker with the coconut oil. 2. In a bowl, whisk the egg white. 3. Add the cinnamon, coconut sugar, vanilla, maple syrup, and salt. Whisk to combine. 4. Add the pecans and stir to coat. Pour the pecans into the slow cooker. 5. Cover the slow cooker and set to low temp setting. Cook for 3 to 4 hours. 6. Remove the pecans from the slow cooker and spread them on a baking sheet or other cooling surface. Let cool for 5 to 10 minutes before serving.

Per Serving: Calories 282; Fat 23g; Sodium 242mg; Carbs 13g; Fiber 1g; Sugar 2g; Protein 9g

Tangy Cran–Apple Pear Compote

Prep time: 10 minutes | Cook time: 6-8 hours | Serves: 4

¾ cup no-sugar-added cranberry juice

¼ cup pure maple syrup

2 medium apples, peeled, cored, and chopped

2 medium pears, peeled, cored, and

chopped

⅓ cup dried cranberries

1 to 1½ cups no-sugar-added vanilla ice cream

1. In a slow cooker, combine the cranberry juice, maple syrup, apples, pears, and dried cranberries. Cover the slow cooker and cook on low temp setting for 6 to 8 hours, until the apples and pears are soft and easily mashed. 2. Serve the compote warm on its own or with ¼ cup of ice cream per serving.

Per Serving: Calories 260; Fat 21g; Sodium 71mg; Carbs 21g; Fiber 10g; Sugar 1g; Protein 11g

Carrot Pudding

Prep time: 20 minutes | Cook time: 5-7 hours | Serves: 12

3 cups finely grated carrots

1½ cups chopped pecans

1 cup golden raisins

1 cup almond flour

1 cup coconut flour

½ cup coconut sugar

1 teaspoon baking powder

1½ teaspoons ground cinnamon

2 eggs, beaten

2 cups canned coconut milk

1. In a slow cooker, mix all of the ingredients. Cover the slow cooker and cook on low temp setting for 5 to 7 hours until the pudding is set. 2. Serve warm, either plain or with softly whipped heavy cream.

Per Serving: Calories 395; Fat 37g; Sodium 105mg; Carbs 13g; Fiber 3g; Sugar 1g; Protein 10g

Cranberry–Pineapple Punch

Prep time: 10 minutes | Cook time: 4 hours | Serves: 8

5 decaf black tea bags

1 cup no-sugar-added orange juice

1 cup no-sugar-added apple juice

2 cups chopped pineapple

5 cups apple cider

1 cup fresh cranberries

Ground cinnamon, for topping

1. In a slow cooker, combine the tea bags, orange juice, apple juice, pineapple, apple cider, and cranberries. Mix well. 2. Cover the slow cooker and cook on low temp setting for 4 hours, until the mixture is warm but not boiling. 3. Discard the tea bags. Serve the punch warm in mugs with a sprinkle of cinnamon on top. If you are in the liquids stage, strain and discard the solids before serving.

Per Serving: Calories 340; Fat 33g; Sodium 17mg; Carbs 7g; Fiber 3g; Sugar 3g; Protein 3g

Vanilla Tapioca Pudding

Prep time: 10 minutes | Cook time: 6 hours | Serves: 12-14

5 cups 2 percent milk

2½ cups heavy (whipping) cream

2½ cups water

1½ cups coconut sugar

1 cup small pearl tapioca

4 eggs, beaten

1 teaspoon vanilla extract

Whipped cream, fresh fruit, cocoa powder, or ground cinnamon, for topping

1. In a slow cooker, combine the milk, cream, water, sugar, tapioca, and eggs. 2. Cover the slow cooker and cook on low temp setting for 6 hours, until thick and creamy. 3. Stir in the vanilla. If you want to serve the pudding chilled, place on a cooling rack. Remove the lid. Let the pudding cool for 20 to 30 minutes. Then, cover and refrigerate for 2 to 3 hours. 4. Serve the pudding warm or chilled with whipped cream, fresh fruit, cocoa powder, or cinnamon.

Per Serving: Calories 129; Fat 11g; Sodium 55mg; Carbs 10g; Fiber 2g; Sugar 1g; Protein 4g

Chocolate-Nut Clusters

Prep time: 10 minutes | Cook time: 2 hours | Serves: 60

4 pounds dairy-free 70% to 80% cacao dark chocolate, chopped

¼ cup coconut oil

2 teaspoons vanilla extract

1 teaspoon ground cinnamon

¼ teaspoon ground cloves

4 cups roasted cashews

3 cups coarsely chopped pecans

1. In a slow cooker, mix the chopped chocolate, coconut oil, vanilla, cinnamon, and cloves. Cover the slow cooker and cook on low temp setting for 2 hours until the chocolate melts. 2. Stir the chocolate mixture until it is smooth. 3. Stir in the cashews and pecans. 4. Drop the mixture by tablespoons onto waxed paper or parchment paper. Let stand until set.

Per Serving: Calories 136; Fat 13g; Sodium 11mg; Carbs 11g; Fiber 5g; Sugar 0g; Protein 2g

Crunchy Coconut Cacao Oats Cookies

Prep time: 15 minutes | Cook time: 1½ hours | Serves: 12

½ cup coconut oil

½ cup unsweetened almond milk

1 overripe banana, mashed well

½ cup coconut sugar

¼ cup cacao powder

1 teaspoon vanilla extract

¼ teaspoon sea salt

3 cups rolled oats

½ cup almond butter

1. In a bowl, stir the coconut oil, almond milk, mashed banana, coconut sugar, cacao powder, vanilla, and salt. Pour the mixture into the slow cooker. 2. Pour the oats on top without stirring. 3. Put the almond butter on top of the oats without stirring. 4. Cover the slow cooker and set to high. Cook for 1½ hours. 5. Stir the mixture well. As it cools, scoop tablespoon-size balls out and press onto a baking sheet to continue to cool. Serve when hardened.

Per Serving: Calories 151; Fat 14g; Sodium 64mg; Carbs 13g; Fiber 3g; Sugar 1g; Protein 2g

Tropical Coconut–Vanilla Yogurt

Prep time: 15 minutes | Cook time: 1-2 hours | Serves: 6

3 (13.5-ounce) cans full-fat coconut milk

5 probiotic capsules

1 teaspoon raw honey

½ teaspoon vanilla extract

1. Pour the coconut milk into the slow cooker. 2. Cover the slow cooker and set to high temp. Cook for 1 to 2 hours, until the temperature of the milk reaches 180°F measured with a candy thermometer. 3. Turn off the slow cooker and allow the temperature of the milk to come down close to 100°F. 4. Open the probiotic capsules and pour in the contents, along with the honey and vanilla. Stir well to combine. 5. Re-cover the slow cooker, turn it off and unplug it, and wrap it in a towel to keep warm overnight as it ferments. 6. Pour the yogurt into sterilized jars and refrigerate. The yogurt should thicken slightly in the refrigerator, where it will keep for up to 1 week.

Per Serving: Calories 103; Fat 7g; Sodium 59mg; Carbs 13g; Fiber 2g; Sugar 1g; Protein 8g

Lemony Cinnamon Apples and Pears

Prep time: 10 minutes | Cook time: 4-6 hours | Serves: 8-10

2 (14½-ounce) cans no-sugar-added sliced pears, drained

4 cups sliced peeled apples (3 or 4 medium apples)

1 tablespoon coconut oil

2 teaspoons lemon juice

1 teaspoon ground cinnamon

1 to 2 tablespoons honey

2 to 2½ cups no-sugar-added vanilla ice cream

1 to 1¼ cups light whipped cream, for topping

1. In a bowl, toss the pears, apples, and coconut oil. Pour into a slow cooker. 2. Add the lemon juice and cinnamon. Stir gently. 3. Gently stir in the honey. Cover the slow cooker and cook on low temp setting for 4 to 6 hours, until the pears and apples are soft. 4. Remove the stoneware crock (inner cooking vessel) and place on a cooling rack. Remove the lid. Let the dessert cool for 20 to 30 minutes, until room temperature. Cover and refrigerate for 2 to 3 hours. 5. Serve the pears and apples chilled with ¼ cup of ice cream per serving or 2 tablespoons of light whipped cream per serving.

Per Serving: Calories 129; Fat 12g; Sodium 75mg; Carbs 9g; Fiber 1g; Sugar 1g; Protein 3g

Nutty Apples

Prep time: 20 minutes | Cook time: 4-6 hours | Serves: 8

8 apples

2 tablespoons freshly squeezed lemon juice

1½ cups buckwheat flakes

1 cup chopped walnuts

⅓ cup coconut sugar

1 teaspoon ground cinnamon

¼ teaspoon salt

6 tablespoons unsalted butter, cut into pieces

½ cup apple juice

1. Peel a strip of skin around the top of each apple to prevent splitting. Carefully remove the apple core, making sure not to cut all the way through to the bottom. Brush the apples with lemon juice and set aside. 2. In a bowl, mix the buckwheat flakes, walnuts, coconut sugar, cinnamon, and salt. 3. Drizzle the melted butter over the buckwheat mixture and mix until crumbly. Use this mixture to stuff the apples, rounding the stuffing on top of each apple. 4. In a slow cooker, place the stuffed apples. Pour the apple juice around the apples. 5. Cover the slow cooker and cook on low temp setting for 4 to 6 hours until the apples are very tender.

Per Serving: Calories 170; Fat 4g; Sodium 84mg; Carbs 15g; Fiber 4g; Sugar 1g; Protein 4g

Prep time: 15 minutes | Cook time: 4 hours | Serves: 5

Grated zest and juice from 1 medium orange

½ cup Mulled Apple Cider, apple cider, or unsweetened apple juice

1 tablespoon maple syrup

5 apples, cored, with a 1-inch strip peeled off around the top

½ cup unsweetened dried cranberries

½ cup unsalted shelled pistachios, chopped

Whipped cream, for serving

1. In a slow cooker, whisk the orange zest and juice, cider, and maple syrup. Place the apples upright in the slow cooker in a single layer. Spoon some of the orange juice mixture from the bottom of the slow cooker over the apples. Stuff the apples with the cranberries and pistachios and let any extra overflow into the pot. 2. Cover the slow cooker and cook on low temp setting for 3½ to 4 hours, until the apples are cooked to liking. They will be crisp-tender after 3½ hours and softer after 4 hours. 3. Transfer the apples to serving bowls and spoon over some of the liquid plus any extra cranberries and pistachios from the bottom of the pot. Top with whipped cream.

Per Serving: Calories 173; Fat 13g; Sodium 394mg; Carbs 9g; Fiber 0g; Sugar 0g; Protein 12g

Conclusion

Thank you for purchasing our cookbook! The Ninja Foodi PossibleCooker PRO is an advanced appliance. It has eight cooking functions: Slow cook, Sear or Sauté, Braise, Sous Vide, Steam, Bake, Proof, and Keep Warm. The cleaning process is very simple. I added cooking time, temperature, and quantity of added-water of each food like veggies, meat, and other. You can prepare any time of meals to use this appliance. In this cookbook, you will get delicious and every type of recipe you want. This appliance is perfect for those who have no time to cook for a long time. Thank you for choosing my book. I hope you love and appreciate my book. This appliance has a large capacity, and you can prepare a large amount of food for your big family. Read a book, appreciate it, and enjoy recipes! If you don't have any knowledge of using this appliance, read this cookbook thoroughly. I hope you will get all answers that come to your mind. Thank you for appreciating us to purchase this cookbook. STAY HAPPY & GOOD LUCK!

Appendix 1 Measurement Conversion Chart

VOLUME EQUIVALENTS (LIQUID)

US STANDARD	US STANDARD (OUNCES)	METRIC (APPROXIMATE)
2 tablespoons	1 fl.oz	30 mL
¼ cup	2 fl.oz	60 mL
½ cup	4 fl.oz	120 mL
1 cup	8 fl.oz	240 mL
1½ cup	12 fl.oz	355 mL
2 cups or 1 pint	16 fl.oz	475 mL
4 cups or 1 quart	32 fl.oz	1 L
1 gallon	128 fl.oz	4 L

VOLUME EQUIVALENTS (DRY)

US STANDARD	METRIC (APPROXIMATE)
⅛ teaspoon	0.5 mL
¼ teaspoon	1 mL
½ teaspoon	2 mL
¾ teaspoon	4 mL
1 teaspoon	5 mL
1 tablespoon	15 mL
¼ cup	59 mL
½ cup	118 mL
1 cup	235 mL
2 cups	475 mL
3 cups	700 mL
4 cups	1 L

FAHRENHEIT (F)	CELSIUS (C) (APPROXIMATE)
225 ℉	107 ℃
250 ℉	120 ℃
275 ℉	135 ℃
300 ℉	150 ℃
325 ℉	160 ℃
350 ℉	180 ℃
375 ℉	190 ℃
400 ℉	205 ℃
425 ℉	220 ℃
450 ℉	235 ℃
475 ℉	245 ℃
500 ℉	260 ℃

US STANDARD	METRIC (APPROXIMATE)
1 ounce	28 g
2 ounces	57 g
5 ounces	142 g
10 ounces	284 g
15 ounces	425 g
16 ounces (1 pound)	455 g
1.5pounds	680 g
2pounds	907 g

Appendix 2 Recipes Index

Printed in Great Britain
by Amazon